WRITERS AND THEIR WORK

ISOBEL ARMSTRONG
General Editor

HENRIK IBSEN

HENRIK IBSEN

Sally Ledger

Second Edition

NORTHCOTE

BRITISH COUNCIL

ATLANTIC
PUBLISHERS & DISTRIBUTORS (P) LTD

This edition is published by

ATLANTIC
PUBLISHERS & DISTRIBUTORS (P) LTD
7/22, Ansari Road, Darya Ganj, New Delhi-110 002
Tel: 40775252, 23273880, 23275880, 23280451; Fax: +91-11-23285873
E-mail: orders@atlanticbooks.com; Web: www.atlanticbooks.com

By arrangement with
Northcote House Publishers Ltd
Horndon House, Horndon, Tavistock, Devon, PL19 9NQ,
United Kingdom. (T)+44(0)1822 810066; (F)+44(0)1822 810034
(E) northcote.house@virgin.net and (W) www.northcotehouse.co.uk
The *Writers and their Work* series is published in association with the British Council.

Second edition 2008
First Indian Reprint 2010
First published in 1999 by Northcote House Publishers Ltd

ISBN 978-81-269-1288-9

For sale in the Indian sub-continent only. Not for export elsewhere.

British Library Cataloguing-in-Publication Data
A catalogue record for this book is available from the British Library

Typeset by PDQ Typesetting, Newcastle-under-Lyme
Printed in India at Nice Printing Press, A-33/3A, Site-IV,
Industrial Area, Sahibabad, Ghaziabad, U.P.

For Bill and Barbara Ledger

Contents

Acknowledgements

I would like to thank Isobel Armstrong for her encouragement and advice, and Angelique Richardson for bibliographical assistance. Special thanks to Josephine McDonagh, who discussed the book with me at various stages, and to Jim Porteous for his support throughout. Birkbeck College English Department kindly provided me with research assistance and a light teaching load in the final stages of the study's preparation. Most of all I would like to say 'thank you' to Bill Greenslade and John Reid, who first introduced me to Ibsen's plays when I worked with them at the University of the West of England.

Biographical Outline

1828 20 March, born in Skien, in south-east Norway, in 1828, the second child of Knud Ibsen, a merchant.

1835 When Ibsen is only 7 years old, his father's business collapses, and the family moves to a smaller house in Venstop, a couple of miles from Skien, where they reside for the next eight years.

1843 27 December, at the age of 15, Ibsen becomes an apothecary's assistant in Grimstad, a tiny port further down the coast from Skien. He works here for six years, living in great poverty.

1846 9 October, at the age of 18, he fathers an illegitimate child with a servant-girl.

1848–9 Writes his first play, *Catiline*, which is rejected by the Christiania Theatre.

1850 28 April, leaves Grimstad in favour of student life in Christiania (now Oslo).

Befriends Björnstjerne Björnson, who is to become his main literary rival in Norway.

26 September, *The Burial Mound* is performed at the Christiania Theatre, the first performance of an Ibsen play.

1851 Joins the National Theatre at Bergen, where he writes, directs, and designs costumes and keeps accounts.

1853 2 January, his comedy, *St John's Night*, is performed at the Bergen Theatre.

1855 2 January, *Lady Inger of Ostraat*, a historical drama, is performed at the Bergen Theatre.

1856 2 January, *The Feast at Solhaug* is performed at the Bergen Theatre, and again on 13 March at Christiania.

1857 2 January, *Olaf Liljekrans* is performed at the Bergen Theatre.

Leaves the Bergen Theatre to become artistic manager of the Norwegian Theatre in Christiania.

1858 18 June, marries Suzannah Thoresen, a strong-minded, educated woman who is a supporter of the women's movement. Their marriage seems to have been stable, although towards the close there are hints in letters (and in Ibsen's last plays) that it was not the most passionately fulfilling of relationships.

24 November, first performance of *The Vikings of Helgeland*, at the Norwegian Christiania Theatre.

1859 23 December, Ibsen's son, Sigurd, is born, his and Suzannah's only child.

1862 1 June, Norwegian Christiania Theatre is declared bankrupt and Ibsen loses his job. For the next two years he has no regular source of income.

1863 October, *The Pretenders* is published.

1864 17 January, *The Pretenders* is performed in Christiania.

September, Ibsen, his wife and child take up residence in Rome. He will live in exile, in Italy and Germany, for the next twenty-seven years.

1866 15 March, *Brand*, a 'dramatic poem', is published in Copenhagen and is well received in Scandinavia.

1867 14 November, *Peer Gynt*, a verse drama, is published in Copenhagen.

1868 October, the Ibsens move to Dresden.

1869 30 September, *The League of Youth*, a prose drama, is published. From now onwards all of Ibsen's plays will be written in prose.

1871 3 May, Ibsen's selected *Poems* are published.

1872 Edmund Gosse reviews Ibsen's *Poems* in the *Spectator*, the first critical discussion of the Norwegian's work in Britain. Over the next two years Gosse will write several more pieces on Ibsen.

1873 16 October, *Emperor and Galilean* published.

1875 ?15 April, moves from Dresden to Munich.

1876 24 February, first performance of *Peer Gynt*, with Grieg's music, at the Christiania Theatre.

1877 11 October, *The Pillars of Society* is published.

1879 4 December, *A Doll's House* is published.

1880 2 November, moves from Munich to Rome, where his son

Sigurd will complete his law studies. Is mainly resident in Rome for the next five years.
15 December, *Quicksands,* an adaptation of *Pillars of Society,* is performed at the Gaiety Theatre, London, the first performance of any Ibsen play on the London stage.

1881 12 December, *Ghosts* is published.

1882 28 November, *An Enemy of the People* is published.

1884 11 November, *The Wild Duck* is published.

1885 Visits Norway for three months in the summer. In October he takes up residence once more in Munich, where he will live for the next six years.

1886 23 November, *Rosmersholm* is published.

1888 28 November, *The Lady from the Sea* is published.

1889 3–15 March, is fêted in Berlin and Weimar, where he attends performances of his plays.
7 June, *A Doll's House* is performed at London Novelty Theatre, the first unbowdlerized British production.

1890 First collected edition of Ibsen's plays in English begins publication under the editorship of William Archer.
December, *Hedda Gabler* is published.

1891 13 March, the Independent Theatre performs *Ghosts* in London, where it causes a scandal.
July–October, visits Norway, and decides to return to his home country to live.

1892 Ibsen's son, Sigurd, marries Björnstjerne Björnson's daughter, Bergliot.
12 December, *The Master Builder* is published.

1893 His first grandchild is born.

1894 December, *Little Eyolf* is published.

1896 12 December, *John Gabriel Borkman* is published.

1898 20 March, Ibsen is congratulated by well-wishers from across the world on his 70th birthday. Collected editions of his works are begun in Norwegian and German. He receives many honours.

1899 19 December, *When We Dead Awaken* is published.

1900 Suffers his first stroke.

1901 Is partly paralysed by a second stroke. Gradually becomes largely helpless.

1906 23 May, dies in Christiania, aged 78, with his wife at his bedside. Twelve thousand mourners attend his funeral.

Note on Translations

I have used Michael Meyer's translations of Ibsen's plays throughout. They are published by Methuen Drama in a uniform paperback edition as follows:

Ibsen, Plays One: Ghosts, The Wild Duck, The Master Builder
Ibsen, Plays Two: A Doll's House, An Enemy of the People, Hedda Gabler
Ibsen, Plays Three: Rosmersholm, Little Eyolf, The Lady from the Sea
Ibsen, Plays Four: John Gabriel Borkman, The Pillars of Society, When We Dead Awaken
Ibsen, Plays Five: Brand, Emperor and Galilean
Ibsen, Plays Six: Peer Gynt and *The Pretenders*

All page references to Ibsen's plays in this study refer to these editions. As well as for the ease of access to students, I have chosen to use these translations of Ibsen's plays for the care Meyer takes to deploy a vocabulary which is largely common both to the late nineteenth century when the plays were written and produced, and to today's theatre audiences at the end of the twentieth century. Meyer nicely captures the quotidian, idiomatic quality of much of Ibsen's dramatic prose from his middle period in particular, as well as reproducing the evasiveness of a good deal of the dialogue in the plays.

Abbreviations

References to Ibsen's plays are to the act number, followed by the page number in the Methuen Drama paperback edition. I have used the following abbreviations:

DH	*A Doll's House*
EP	*An Enemy of the People*
G	*Ghosts*
HG	*Hedda Gabler*
B	*John Gabriel Borkman*
LE	*Little Eyolf*
LS	*The Lady from the Sea*
PG	*Peer Gynt*
R	*Rosmersholm*
WWDA	*When We Dead Awaken*

1

Ibsenism and *A Doll's House*

> Ibsen's message to you is – if you are a member of society, defy it; if you have a duty, violate it, if you have a sacred tie, break it, if you have a religion, stand on it instead of crouching under it; if you have bound yourself by a promise or an oath, cast them to the winds; if the lust of self-sacrifice seize you, wrestle with it as with the devil; and if, in spite of all, you cannot resist the temptation to be virtuous, go drown yourself before you have time to waste the lives of all about you with the infection of that fell disease. Here at last is a call to arms with some hope in it![1]

So wrote George Bernard Shaw in an 1890 Fabian Lecture on Ibsen, claiming the Norwegian as the leader of a vanguard of 'modern' Victorians who at the fin de siècle championed socialism, feminism and new forms of artistic expression. And yet Ibsen, as a Scandinavian, was no Victorian. Astonishingly, given the profound cultural influence he exerted on late-nineteenth-century London, the Norwegian playwright never set foot on British soil. Despite his bodily absence, Ibsen's impact on Victorian cultural modernity in the 1880s and 1890s was immense. On 7 June 1889, the first unbowdlerized production of *A Doll's House* was performed at London's Novelty Theatre. It was attended by a dazzling array of bohemians and intellectuals including Bernard Shaw, who was subsequently to become one of the Norwegian's most significant publicists in England. Eleanor Marx (the daughter of Karl), one of the first to translate Ibsen's plays into English, and other metropolitan feminists and novelists such as Olive Schreiner, Edith Lees Ellis and Emma Frances Brooke, were also there. This was not the usual London theatre audience which would have attended the mainstream productions of comedies, romances and melodramas which had dominated the English theatre throughout much of the Victorian period. Writing thirty years after the London première of *A Doll's House,* the writer Edith Lees Ellis wrote how:

> A few of us collected outside the theatre breathless with excitement. Olive Schreiner was there and Dolly Radford the poetess...Emma Brooke...and Eleanor Marx. We were restive and almost savage in our arguments. What did it mean?...Was it life or death for women?...Was it joy or sorrow for men? That a woman should demand her own emancipation and leave her husband and children in order to get it, savoured less of sacrifice than sorcery.[2]

What was clear was that something had 'happened' to the theatre in England, and that it would never be the same again. In 1886 the playwright Henry Arthur Jones had acknowledged that 'there is no drama that even pretends to picture modern English life; I might also say that pretends to picture human life at all'.[3] But all this changed in 1889 with the arrival of *A Doll's House* in London, a performance which constituted a watershed in the evolution of British theatre. Ibsen did for European drama what Flaubert had done for the novel back in 1856; he introduced a 'new realism' to the stage which, with its critical scrutiny of the lives and values of the bourgeois classes, involved a wholesale rejection of the romantic plots which had prevailed in a good deal of British drama as well as fiction for a large part of the nineteenth century.

Eleanor Marx, who was to become one of London's leading 'Ibsenites', had written to her friend Havelock Ellis in 1885 that 'I feel I must do something to make people understand our Ibsen a little more than they do'.[4] Accordingly, Marx sent out invitations to a 'few people worth reading *Nora* to', and on 15 January 1886, in their flat in Great Russell Street, Marx and her common-law husband, Edward Aveling, hosted a reading of *A Doll's House* in the reliable Henrietta Frances Lord translation. George Bernard Shaw took the role of the blackmailing bank clerk, Krogstad, and William Morris's daughter May played the long-suffering Christine Linde; Eleanor Marx took the lead with Nora Helmer, whilst Edward Aveling played the chauvinistic and hypocritical husband, Torvald Helmer. This private performance of *A Doll's House* proved to be an auspicious occasion for what emerged in the 1880s and 1890s as 'Ibsenism', a political and cultural formation consisting of Marxists, socialists, Fabians and feminists, who jointly hailed Ibsen as spokesman for their various causes. Eleanor Marx regarded Ibsen as a herald of change, both recording and contributing to what she hoped would be a catastrophic implosion of the bourgeois social fabric. George Bernard Shaw regarded him as a morally decisive realist whose radical agenda for social change Shaw articulated fully in his highly influential long essay *The Quintessence of Ibsenism* (1891). Ibsen's status as a radical icon endured well into the twentieth century, with a writer for the *Bookman* in 1913 acclaiming Nora Helmer as an early New Woman – 'woman "new" enough to do the *Freewoman* criticisms of H. G. Wells's latest novels!'[5]

Not everyone responded to Ibsen's work so enthusiastically, though. The same London première of *A Doll's House* which so enthused the English capital's early socialists and feminists outraged more conservative commentators. Clement Scott, the theatre critic for the reactionary *Daily Telegraph*, signalled his future role as Ibsen's bitterest critical enemy in England when he reviewed the Novelty Theatre's first night production of *A Doll's House*. Scott, whilst impressed by the profound concentration displayed by the first night audience – 'The interest was so intense last night that a pin might have been heard to drop' – was of the opinion that the play would not appeal to most decent-minded English theatre audiences: 'We do not honestly believe that those theories as expressed in *The Doll's House* [sic] would ever find favour with the great body of English playgoers'. The reason for this was the rotten morality, as Scott saw it, that the play promulgated. Like most of Ibsen's opponents, Scott was outraged by Nora Helmer's desertion of her children, incredulous that she would '[abandon] her innocent children, and [become] absolutely inhuman, simply because she discovers her husband is an egotist and that she has been a petted little fool'.[6] In a subsequent review Scott reflected on this 'unnatural... creature' that 'A cat or dog would tear any one who separated it from its offspring, but the socialistic Nora, the apostle of the new creed of humanity, leaves her children almost without a pang. She has determined to leave her home. ...It is all self, self, self! This is the ideal woman of the new creed.'[7] The 'new creed' was 'Ibsenism', and Ibsenism sounded the death knell for those 'Victorian Values' which had been so pervasive in Britain throughout the second half of the nineteenth century.

Born and bred in Norway, Ibsen lived for the greater part of his adult life in Italy and Germany. His cosmopolitanism is important, for it took a relative outsider to break through what we now describe as 'Victorian Values' and produce plays which challenged the status quo, critically dissecting 'modern' life and all its problems. Ibsen paved the way for other iconoclastic and anti-establishment writers in Britain such as George Bernard Shaw, Thomas Hardy, and a whole host of 'New Woman' novelists, trailing a blaze through the cultural codes of the British establishment and finding himself acclaimed as an 'advanced' and emphatically 'modern' phenomenon.

Although first performed in London in 1889, Ibsen had actually written *A Doll's House* ten years before. In 1879, though, Victorian England was not ready for his work. In 1884 a much diluted and heavily 'cut' adaptation of the play was performed in London. The play, rather coyly entitled *Breaking a Butterfly*, was written by Henry Arthur Jones and Henry Herman; it transposed Ibsen's radically subversive play into a banal exposition of moral trivia. In the adaptation, Torvald Helmer (renamed Philip Goddard) becomes a positively saintly husband, amply forgiving Nora for her deceptions and heroically taking the blame for her financial fraud upon his own shoulders. Nora, worshipping at the feet of this model of Victorian masculinity, is shown to be prettily repentant for her past indiscretions, and eternally grateful to her husband for his protection of her against their consequences. In *Breaking a Butterfly*, Victorian gender codes, instead of being overturned (as they are in *A Doll's House*), are enthusiastically reinforced. The husband takes the moral lead, cushioning his helpless, butterfly-like wife from the realities of the harsh economic and social world, teaching her that her proper place is in the home, not bothering her pretty head with matters financial. Dr Rank, who is a rather sombre presence in *A Doll's House*, disappears altogether, whilst Krogstad, who is actually quite a complex social pariah in Ibsen's play, becomes an ordinary villain from a melodrama. The play ends with a predictably saccharine reconciliation between husband and wife. William Archer, a reviewer, critic and leading translator of Ibsen, remarked in a of *Breaking a Butterfly* that 'The adapters... have felt it ...rul to eliminate all that was satirical or unpleasant, and in making their work sympathetic, they at once made it trivial. I am the last to blame them for doing so. Ibsen on the English stage is impossible.'[8]

A Doll's House may have been 'impossible' on the English stage until 1889, but Ibsen had conceived some of the ideas for the play many years before. The model for Nora Helmer was a young Norwegian woman, Laura Kieler, who admired Ibsen's plays and had written a proto-feminist novel called *Brand's Daughters* in response to one of his early plays, *Brand* (1866). Ibsen had corresponded with Laura Kieler (then Petersen) in 1870, and met her in Dresden in 1871. They had got on very well, and he had affectionately referred to her as his 'skylark'. She re-entered his life in 1876, three years before he published *A Doll's House*; in the intervening years, she had married a Danish schoolteacher, and the marriage was not going well. She confided to Ibsen's wife Suzannah that her husband had contracted tuberculosis and that she had been advised to take him to a warmer climate. They had little money, and Victor Kieler became neurotically hysterical at the merest mention of their financial position. Laura had secretly obtained a loan to fund a trip to Italy; the warmer weather did its work, and her husband would go on to live for a further forty years. In 1878 the loan was recalled, and in a frantic attempt to raise funds Laura Kieler sent Ibsen a manuscript of a novel she had written, begging him to recommend it to his publisher. Ibsen thought it was a terrible novel, and urged her in a letter to confide to her husband all the details of the loan she had taken out on his behalf. On receipt of the letter Laura, in despair, burned the manuscript of the novel and forged a cheque to repay the loan. The forgery was discovered, and she was, after all, forced to tell the whole story to her husband. He, regardless of the fact that the borrowed money had been spent on him, told her she was unworthy to have charge of their children. When she subsequently suffered a nervous breakdown, he committed her to a public asylum, and demanded a legal separation in order to get the children away from her. After being incarcerated for a month, Laura managed to get discharged from the asylum and begged her husband to take her back. He grudgingly agreed.[9] It was from this rather tragic raw material that Ibsen wrought *A Doll*[...] imaginatively transforming the broken Laura Kieler in[...] woman determined to discover her own identity and thereby to create a new life for herself, unhampered by her narrow, egotistical husband. *A Doll's House* is a bold attempt imaginatively to emancipate Laura Kieler from the cowed, subordinate position of disgraced wife, and to metamorphose her into a New Woman with a desire for independence and a full inner life of her own. Laura Kieler didn't thank Ibsen for his play, though. The identity of the original for Nora Helmer was soon to become common knowledge, but whilst *A Doll's House* made Ibsen famous it brought Kieler no joy.[10]

In October 1878, in Rome, Ibsen was clearly contemplating the writing of *A Doll's House,* although he didn't start work on it properly until the beginning of May 1879. In his 'Notes For a Modern Tragedy' (19 October 1878), he reflected that:

> A woman cannot be herself in modern society. It is an exclusively male society, with laws made by men and with prosecutors and judges who assess feminine conduct from a masculine standpoint.
>
> She has committed forgery, and is proud of it; for she has done it out of love for her husband, to save his life. But this husband of hers takes his standpoint, conventionally honourable, on the side of the law, and sees the situation with male eyes.[11]

One of the hallmarks of Ibsen's middle and later plays is a rebellion against the stifling and as he saw it petty morality of provincial bourgeois life in nineteenth-century Norway. Writing in 1878 to his sometime friend and erstwhile rival, the Norwegian novelist and playwright Björnson, Ibsen had condemned the 'prejudice and narrow mindedness and short-sightedness and subservience and unthinking trust in authority' which he found characteristic of his native country.[12] Ibsen's attack on such narrowness in *A Doll's House* struck a strong chord with the bohemian, intellectual audience which attended the London première in 1889. The morality of provincial Norway in the nineteenth century had a curious resonance, it would seem, with the bourgeois moral codes of late-Victorian London.

A Doll's House is one of Ibsen's so-called 'realist problem plays' written between 1877 and 1882 (the others are *The Pillars of Society* (1877), *Ghosts* (1881) and *An Enemy of the People* (1882)). In

herself to be in control of her own destiny, and to be living in the real, material world where she is capable of making rational decisions. Never before has she had the opportunity to discard – if only momentarily – her doll-like existence as Torvald's pretty little wife. As she explains to her husband in the final, harrowing scene of the play, hitherto she has merely been a cipher and an object of exchange between her father and her husband:

> When I lived with papa, he used to tell me what he thought about everything, so that I never had any opinion but his. And if I did have any of my own, I kept them quiet, because he wouldn't have liked them. He called me his little doll, and he played with me just the way I played with my dolls. Then I came here to live in your house –. . . I mean, I passed from papa's hands into yours. You arranged everything the way you wanted it, so that I simply took over your taste in everything – or pretended I did – I don't really know – I think it was a little of both – first one and then the other. . . . You and papa have done me a great wrong. It's your fault that I have done nothing with my life.' (*DH* III, 98)

It is interesting here that Nora is conscious of a process of repression, whereby she has suppressed her own opinions and tastes to suit those of, firstly, her father, and, secondly, her husband. It is only by freeing herself from the masculine yoke of her doll's-house existence at the close of the play that she can begin to give voice to her repressed ideas and opinions and discover who, when she is allowed to stand alone, she really is (or might be).

It is Christine Linde who acts as a catalyst for Nora's rebellion. It is to Linde that Nora reveals the true state of affairs in her marriage, and this is, significantly, after Christine has openly described her own loveless marriage to a man whom she married purely on the basis that he seemed to be able to provide financial security for herself and her impoverished family. Christine has, since her husband's death, been forced to live an independent life, and from this vantage point she is able to identify the rotten foundations of Nora's marriage. Christine, a woman who knows the misery of an unhappy marriage, insists that Nora should tell the truth to Torvald about the debt she has incurred on his behalf, believing that it is only through such openness that the marriage can be set onto firmer, more solid foundations. Ibsen, it would seem, entirely endorses Christine's viewpoint (hers is, after all, the same kind of advice he gave to Laura Kieler in 1878).

Many students of *A Doll's House* have wondered at Nora's long-standing complicity with her marriage. She has, after all, borne Torvald Helmer three children, and has played the part of an adoring, squirrel-like wife for eight years before discovering that she cannot tolerate such a life. For patriarchy to be effective, though, women *have* to be partially complicit with it – it 'takes two to tango', so to speak. Part of Nora actively *desires* to comply with patriarchal social arrangements. When fretting over her debts, she admits to Christine that she has '[sat] here and imagine[d] some rich old gentleman had fallen in love with me – ... And now... he'd died and when they opened his will it said in big letters: "Everything I possess is to be paid forthwith to my beloved Mrs Nora Helmer in cash"'(*DHI*, 37). Part of Nora would like to live out a patriarchal fantasy, where all material cares are lifted from her shoulders and borne by benevolently paternal men. She is rudely awakened from the fantasy when her own husband is revealed as a selfish coward who has no intention of shouldering even the smallest part of the burden of her financial mistakes. Once roused from her torpor, she determines to take control of her life once and for all.

Helmer's vain, petty and weak character is revealed to the audience well before the final denouement, in his dealings with Krogstad. Krogstad, who desperately needs work at the bank where Helmer is to be vice-president, is denied a job because, as Helmer tells Nora, they knew each other at school, and Krogstad continues to call him by his first name, failing to show the respect to which the banker feels he is entitled. To such pettiness is added cowardice in his response to Krogstad's blackmailing. This, as well as his failure to perceive his own wife's moral strength, indicates a pusillanimous subservience to social convention which eventually blights his marriage. Instead of thanking her for having saved his life, Helmer regards Nora's fiscal indebtedness as a moral weakness. In a fit of self-pity, he reflects on the way, as he sees it, that he is 'condemned to humiliation and ruin simply for the weakness of a woman' (*DH* III, 93–4). It is only at the end of the play that he begins to glimpse the woman whom Nora will become as she rises from the ashes of their marriage.

The only character in the play truly to appreciate Nora's qualities is Dr Rank, a friend of the family. A bachelor who cannot marry because of the syphilis he has inherited from his philandering father, Rank has a symbolic function in the play. The absence of romantic fulfilment and of domestic happiness in his life, and the cause of this (a father who was a faithless husband), mean that Rank symbolises the degeneration of the family, a motif that is central both to *A Doll's House* and to so many other plays by Ibsen (*Ghosts* and *Little Eyolf* to name but two). It is ironic, then, that it is only Rank who seems to 'know' Nora. Deeply and unselfishly in love with her, he suggests to Helmer, after the party and before making his final exit, that Nora need not wear fancy dress for the next 'masquerade' they attend, but that she 'need only appear as her normal, everyday self' (*DH*III, 90). Rank, it seems, has seen through the 'masquerade' of Nora's marriage to Helmer, and much prefers Nora herself to the prettily dressed doll she presents to her husband. In his frequent visits to the Helmers' home he has proved himself to be Nora's only true companion; she is much more 'natural' in his presence than around her husband. When he goes away to die, Nora is left by herself in the marriage, and it is significant that at this point she walks out.

The final slamming of the door at the end of *A Doll's House* is a justly famous dramatic denouement. A good deal of the rest of the play is, though, very discursive, and this is one of the hallmarks of Ibsen's realist drama from his middle period. None the less, the play does not lack dramatic tension and excitement. Nora's terror as she tries to divert her husband from the letter box into which, at any moment, she expects Krogstad's blackmailing letter to drop, is forcefully conveyed to the audience as she bangs on the piano, frantically rehearsing the opening bars of the tarantella she will later perform so hysterically to her husband. The mad, frenzied dance itself is a theatrically forceful manifestation of Nora's desperate plight. Dressed up like an erotic little doll to please her husband, this young woman, unable to speak on her own behalf, unable to express herself to her husband in words, resorts to a hysterical, near-demoniac dance in order to give vent to the complex feelings of helplessness and frustration which now assault her on all sides. The dance releases an almost unbearable tension in the play, which Ibsen has built up in a number of ways. His enclosure of the play's dramatic action in a single room, and Nora's inclusion in every scene, effectively create a stifling atmosphere from which it becomes increasingly imperative that she should attempt to break free. Her continual juggling of visitors, her attempts to prevent Krogstad from making contact with her husband in his own house, and her intense efforts to conceal information from Torvald, all contribute to a mounting dramatic tension which is released in the 'Tarantella' scene. It is only after such a release that Nora can confront her husband openly, and confront at the same time the ruins of her marriage.

In the final scene, Nora takes off her fancy-dress costume, and in so doing divests herself of her 'doll-like' role. The role-playing stops here; Nora can begin to construct an authentic identity for herself. She begins by insisting that her husband engages with her in their first 'serious talk together' in eight years of marriage (*DH* III, 97). Ibsen specialized, in his middle and late plays, in the intense verbal dissection of human relationships with which *A Doll's House* closes. The romantic denouements of theatrical comedy and of the Victorian novel are displaced by a clinical scrutiny of failed romantic alliances. Initially Torvald attempts to sustain a conventional line on Nora's behaviour, reprovingly reminding her that a woman's 'most sacred duties' are towards her husband and children. When she demurs, he accuses her of insanity (and a number of other troublesome female characters in nineteenth-century literature are coded as 'lunatics', not least Bertha Mason in Charlotte Brontë's *Jane Eyre* and Lucy Audley in Mary Braddon's *Lady Audley's Secret*). 'Nora, you're ill. You're feverish. I almost believe you're out of your mind', Torvald declares (*DH* III, 101). But Nora is neither a child – not any more, at least – nor insane. She has simply stopped playing a part, and has resolved to focus – for once – on her duty to herself as a responsible adult.

The slamming of the door at the end of *A Doll's House* has a justly prominent place in theatre history. But although the door firmly closes, there is no closure at the play's end. Edith Lees Ellis's questions, posed after the London première of the play, remain pertinent: 'Was it life or death for women? . . . Was it joy or sorrow for men?' These questions remain unanswered after Nora has left her marital home. Late-Victorian critics of the play in England were perturbed by the play's refusal to provide any answers to the questions that it posed. Having walked out of her marriage, what would become of Nora? And what of her husband and her children? These were some of the questions to which critics demanded answers. The desire for a clear-cut moral closure to the play resulted in a number of moralistic sequels. Most notable of these was Walter Besant's 'The Doll's House – and After', in which he imagines the plight of Nora's family twenty-five years after she has walked out on them. Torvald is drunk, dissolute and unemployed, and of the two sons, one is also an alcoholic who can barely hold down a job, and the other is an embezzler. The daughter is a pure young girl who is forced to break off her engagement to a banker's son because of the shame of having a ne'er-do-well father and a mother who deserted them all. The mother, Nora, has become a cold and hard New Woman writer who 'wrote novels ... which the old-fashioned regarded with horror. In them she advocated the great principle of abolishing the family, and making love the sole rule of conduct.'[13] She has a bad moral reputation, and her grown-up daughter refuses Nora's offer of a home. As Nora is driven in her carriage to the railway station, she sees her daughter's dead body being hauled from the river. Christine Linde implores Nora to pause and to consider the suffering she has inflicted on her family, to acknowledge 'The ruin wrought by your own hand. They are bearing home the body of your daughter. She has drowned herself. For her mother's sake – for her father's sake – she has been robbed of her lover. She is dead.'[14] Nora, though, disclaims responsibility, and agrees with her driver's request that they hurry along so as not to miss the train.

Walter Besant's moralistic condemnation of Nora's actions provoked a sharp rejoinder from George Bernard Shaw, who wrote a much more radical response to Nora's abandonment of her marriage in his own sequel, 'Still After the Doll's House: A Sequel to Mr. Besant's Sequel to Henrik Ibsen's Play'.[15] Eleanor Marx and Israel Zangwill joined in the fun with their heavily satirical sequel called *'A Doll's House Repaired'*, in which Nora returns and comically over-acts the part of sweetly repentant errant wife. Instead of Nora slamming the front door, at the end of their humorous sequel Torvald flounces out of the room and huffily slams the bedroom door.

The desire for aesthetic closure is very strong – many students of *A Doll's House* ask the question 'What happened next?' The slamming of the door at the close of the play constituted a refusal to comply with the usual theatrical conventions with which a nineteenth-century theatre audience would have been familiar. Ibsen's theatrical innovation will be the subject of the next chapter.

2

Ibsen, Realism and 'Modern' Drama: From Norwegian Nationalism to *Ghosts*

That Henrik Ibsen should have become one of the giants of modern European drama is little short of astonishing. Born in a small Norwegian town, Skien, before the start of Queen Victoria's reign, Ibsen, the son of a merchant fallen on hard times, had a relatively thin literary tradition on which to draw. The national literature of nineteenth-century Norway was quite slender, the only writer with a 'high-cultural' reputation – Ludvig Holberg (1684–1754) – being long dead. Norway's main literary project when Ibsen was a young man was a nationalistic reclamation of old Norwegian ballads and folktales. It was Ibsen's involvement with this project which would delay his reinvention of European drama.

On his arrival in Christiania (now Oslo) in 1850 as a 22-year-old student, Ibsen quickly got to know the young Björnstjerne Björnson, who would become both a friend and a rival.[1] For both men, the mid-century proved to be an uninspiring time for would-be playwrights. In 1851 Ibsen took up the post of 'dramatic author' at the Bergen Theatre, where he was to spend six years of poverty and artistic depression. He assisted in the production of many popular mid-century plays, but there was (for example) no classical drama, no Shakespeare, and no Molière; nothing, in short, that Ibsen could learn anything new from. High tragedy, comedy, farce and melodrama dominated the Bergen Theatre in the 1850s, and such a dramatic diet was common across much of Europe at this time. 'Serious' drama was never written in prose, and it was always concerned with people of high estate. The idea that a tragedy could be written in prose, or that it could be about ordinary nineteenth-century people, was unheard of. Any such play would not have been considered 'art' by either actors or audience. The theatrical status quo which reigned in the mid-century European theatre would, eventually, be radically dismantled by Ibsen; but this was many years in the future.

Ibsen's first few plays had historical settings and drew on well-worn dramatic traditions. Of his early work, *Catiline* (1849) is a tragedy set in ancient Rome, and is written in rhymed verse. *Lady Inger of Ostraat* (1854) is the first of Ibsen's plays to be written entirely in prose, but it is set in the Norway of 1528, has as its central character a rich noblewoman, and is full of rather clichéd theatrical devices such as mistaken identities, overheard conversations and long monologues, all of which were routinely demanded of mid-nineteenth-century 'tragedy'. *The Feast at Solhaug* (1855) is a balladic comedy, partly rhymed verse, partly prose, and is set in fourteenth-century Norway. It has a less than subtle plot, weak characterization, and is strongly influenced by those Norwegian folk ballads which were being so enthusiastically rediscovered by mid-nineteenth-century Norwegian literary nationalists, with whose ideas Ibsen dallied for a number of years.[2]

In 1857 Ibsen accepted the post of artistic director at the Norwegian Theatre in Christiania, a nationalistic rival to the more established 'Danish' Christiania Theatre. In this same year he completed *The Vikings of Helgeland* (1857), a drama set in tenth-century Norway, and conceived after reading N. M. Petersen's translation of the Icelandic Sagas. Although, like the Sagas themselves, it is an impressive piece of writing, the remoteness of the ancient, heroic figures and the conventions which governed their lives, mean it is a piece of elevated pastiche rather than an actable play in the modern sense. Ibsen's contemporary, Björnson, was frustrated by the play, complaining of Ibsen's Vikings that 'I can't believe that people who lived then were superhuman and godlike. No, damn it, they were human!'[3] Björnson, before Ibsen it seems, had an inkling of the demands of a new, 'modern' drama: what was needed was not remote figures from a distant past, but living and breathing contemporary characters who lived in the world of the everyday. Michael Meyer has commented interestingly on the comparisons which can be made between Ibsen's and James Joyce's development respectively as modern' writers. As he puts it:

> One is reminded of the young James Joyce, fifty years later, similarly caught up in the toils of nationalism which diverted his genius, and who, likewise, was not to fulfil himself until he had escaped from it into self-imposed exile.[4]

Ibsen finally left Norway two plays later, in 1864 (*Love's Comedy*, a play in rhymed verse, was published in 1862, and *The Pretenders*, set in thirteenth-century Norway, appeared in 1863). He travelled to Berlin, Vienna and then across the Alps, eventually reaching Rome. Ibsen's extended residence in Italy and Germany was to revolutionize his dramatic writing. Camilla Collett, the Norwegian feminist, wrote in 1854 of the narrow provincialism of Christiania (Oslo). 'O great and little city!' she lamented, 'You have all the consuming passions, yearnings and pretensions of a great city; and yet you are so small, and so petty, that you cannot gratify one of them'.[5] Once Ibsen was in Italy, he could contemplate both the passions and the pettiness of his native country from a distance, and in so doing managed to extricate himself from the nationalism which until this period had limited his dramatic output. Many years later, in 1898, he recalled his first sight of Italy as he crossed the Alps:

> I...crossed the Alps on 9 May [1864]. Over the high mountains the clouds hung like great, dark curtains, and beneath these we drove through the tunnel and, suddenly, found ourselves at Mira Mara, where that marvellously bright light which is the beauty of the south suddenly revealed itself to me, gleaming like white marble. It was to affect all my later work, even if the content thereof was not always beautiful.

He described his emotion at that time as 'a feeling of being released from the darkness into light, emerging from mists through a tunnel into the sunshine!'[6]

The first play Ibsen wrote in Italy was *Brand* (1866), the second drama in an epic quartet, which had begun with *The Pretenders* and which would also eventually comprise *Peer Gynt* (1867) and *Emperor and Galilean* (1873). A grandiose epic verse tragedy, *Lear-*

like in its focus on a lonely, wayward and spiritually unhappy man, *Brand* was apprehended by its Scandinavian readers as an attack on conventional religion, on patriotism and on conventional social relations, and in this way it anticipates the great, realistic prose dramas of Ibsen's middle period. Like a number of Ibsen's plays, *Brand* was not written with performance in mind, thus liberating the playwright from the limitations of nineteenth-century stagecraft. In this second respect, then, *Brand* is more akin to the fantastical *Peer Gynt*, written in 1867, than to Ibsen's later drama.

It is not until *The League of Youth* (1869) that Ibsen the realist, with whom playgoers and students are now most familiar, announces himself on the European stage. This is Ibsen's first attempt to write a play entirely in modern colloquial dialogue. Conscious that this was a new dramatic departure, he wrote to his publisher, Hegel, that 'It will be in prose, and written entirely with the stage in mind'.[7] In preparing the play, Ibsen asked Hegel to send him regular copies of *Dagbladet*, a Norwegian newspaper, 'not to satisfy an idle curiosity for news... but because I shall thereby be drawn more closely and intensively into life in Norway, and thus feel strengthened for my work'.[8] It is highly significant that Ibsen used contemporary newspapers as a source for his 'realist' prose dramas. Never a bookish playwright, the absence of any sense that he was writing within an established literary tradition surely provides a partial explanation for his ability to invent a new, 'modern' drama in the late nineteenth century. The lack of a literary tradition, which had in his earlier years left him floundering in a nationalistic morass of Norwegian ballads and folktales, enabled him, once he had left Norway's literary milieu behind, to begin afresh, and devise his own dramatic aesthetic based on a literary realism which would wield an enormous influence across Europe well into the twentieth century. A review in the Norwegian *Morgenbladet* (17 October 1869) recognized the aesthetic importance of *The League of Youth*, remarking that 'This latest work marks a new and significant phase in the author's artistic development, a step forward... He places us slap in the midst of real life, where we meet people who are unquestionably of flesh and blood, people such as we unfortunately meet everyday.'[9]

The realism of *The League of Youth* is somewhat undermined by Ibsen's continuing dependence on old-fashioned dramatic conventions (subplots depending on misdirected letters, overheard conversations and other dramatic contrivances), and in this respect it is a transitional work. *The Pillars of Society* (1877) and *A Doll's House* (1879), written within the next decade, were greatly to extend Ibsen's new realist technique, and in both plays his ability to differentiate between various characters' modes of speech makes great headway, a technique which he supremely contributed to modern prose drama. Even more than this, his recurrent focus on a narrow bourgeois provincialism which warps the lives of his central dramatic characters was firmly to establish him as one of the most subversive modern critics of middle-class life in the nineteenth century, a reputation which won him both friends and enemies. Henry James approved this 'new' Ibsen, and reflected on the Norwegian's contribution to European drama thus:

> Ibsen is massively common and 'middle-class,' but neither his spirit nor his manner is small. He is never trivial and never cheap... the operation of talent without glamour... the ugly interior on which his curtain inexorably rises and which, to be honest, I like for the queer associations it has taught us to respect: the hideous carpet and wall paper (one may answer for them), the conspicuous stove, the lonely central table, the 'lamps with green shades'... the pervasive air of small interests and standards, the sign of limited local life.[10]

In a letter to Björnson, written on 12 July 1878, Ibsen had condemned Norwegian 'prejudice and narrow-mindedness and short-sightedness and subservience and unthinking trust in authority'.[11] Such a condemnation had drawn criticism from his countrymen as well as from the wider European literary establishment on the publication of *The Pillars of Society* and *A Doll's House*. Ibsen's popularity, though, had survived his increasingly 'subversive' cultural identity in the late 1870s. But the publication of *Ghosts* in 1881 put him beyond the pale of conventional social and literary codes; the Norwegian's notoriety was now confirmed. *Ghosts*, Ibsen's great naturalist play, greatly damaged not only his reputation but also his pocket; as it began to appear on bookshelves, sales of his plays, on which he depended for his bread and butter, began to plummet.

Ibsen had described *Ghosts* to his publisher as 'a domestic drama in three acts'.[12] But domestic life as it is represented in the play is morally contaminated and thoroughly dysfunctional; it was a type of domesticity which Western Europe in the late nineteenth century wished not to acknowledge. Published in 1881, the play was quickly banned across most of the European continent, its dissection of the inheritance of syphilis and its perceived attack on the traditional bourgeois family proving too much for most national authorities.

Ghosts is the story of a woman (Mrs Alving) who leaves her husband but who is then persuaded by a cleric with whom she is in love (Pastor Manders) to return home. She bears her morally depraved husband a son (Osvald), who turns out to have inherited his father's syphilis. The play not only attacks the sanctity of marriage (a crime of which *A Doll's House* was already guilty), but it also denies the duty of a son to honour his father – a significant violation of the moral codes of a patriarchal society. Whilst his mother 'cling[s] to that old superstition' about a child's duty to his parents, Osvald Alving rejects his father's memory, reflecting that 'I never knew anything about father. I don't remember anything about him, except that once he made me sick' (GIII, 92). Far worse than all this, though, was the play's unmistakable references (if not by name) to venereal disease, its defence of 'free love' and its contemplation of incestuous relationships. This play was, in 1881, moral dynamite.

Like *A Doll's House*, the theatrical realism of *Ghosts* is indicated by Ibsen's detailing of the stage set at the start of Act I:

> *A spacious garden-room, with a door in the left-hand wall and two doors in the right-hand wall. In the centre of the room is a round table with chairs around it; on the table are books, magazines and newspapers. Downstage left is a window, in front of which is a small sofa with a sewing-table by it. Backstage the room opens out into a slightly narrower conservatory, with walls of large panes of glass. In the right-hand wall of the conservatory is a door leading down to the garden. Through the glass wall a gloomy fjord landscape is discernible, veiled by steady rain.*

The spaciousness of the garden room, the books and the magazines, all suggest the comfortable bourgeois status of the Alving family. The domestic nature of the drama is indicated by the sewing table. The gloominess of the fjord and the dreary weather both intimate the general tenor of the drama to follow.

The realistic effect was essential as far as Ibsen was concerned. 'The effect of the play', he wrote, 'depends a great deal on making the spectator feel as if he were actually sitting, listening and looking at events happening in real life.'[13]

The feminine presence of Mrs Alving is suggested in the initial stage directions by the needlework on the table by the sofa. And yet Mrs Alving is no conventional domestic woman. Not only has she, in the past, left her now-dead husband; she also reads 'modern' literature of a morally advanced kind – 'these loathsome, rebellious, free-thinking books!' as Pastor Manders describes them in Act II (p. 62). Mrs Alving is a portrait of what Nora Helmer, the heroine of *A Doll's House*, might have become had she stayed with her husband and children instead of slamming the door on her domestic life. Ibsen had been begged to write a sequel to *A Doll's House* and, arguably, *Ghosts* is that sequel. Writing to Countess Sophie Aldersparre on 24 June 1882, Ibsen remarked that 'I *had* to write *Ghosts*. I couldn't stop at *A Doll's House*; after Nora, I had to create Mrs Alving.'[14] Mrs Alving's decisiveness and moral courage are signalled by her earlier attempt to leave her husband whatever the social outcry. It is only because the man she loves, Pastor Manders, insists she return to her marital home that she relents, a decision which she lives bitterly to regret. She has spent a life nursing an increasingly debauched and diseased husband, sending her son away from home to protect him from the morally contaminating influence of his father. In the period of her husband's physical decline, she has run the family estate single-handedly, taking on traditionally 'masculine' responsibilities and shielding her family from moral shame.

At the time of the action of the play, Mrs Alving's main project is the opening of an orphanage built in her husband's name. Anxious that Osvald should inherit nothing from his dead father – not even his money – Mrs Alving spends this inheritance on the orphanage. The grotesque irony is, of course, that whilst economic and even social inheritance can be externally controlled – by removing him from his father's influence she has ensured that Osvald has led a morally temperate life, and has her own progressive and forward-looking social ideals – biological inheritance is unavoidable. He may not inherit his father's money, but Osvald does inherit his father's syphilis.

The influence of heredity theory, which was highly influential in the late nineteenth century, is pronounced in *Ghosts*. This quasi-scientific biological theory owed a lot to the work of Charles Darwin (with which Ibsen became familiar), and to the more general current of thought in the nineteenth century which is known as Social Darwinism. Few would dispute Charles Darwin's status as a giant of modernity. But the category of the modern, in relation both to Darwin's thought and, more specifically, in relation to the impact of Darwin's thought on Ibsen's plays, is profoundly problematic. For heredity theory has an intensely *regressive* effect on Ibsen's drama, halting the tide of modernity which the Nora Helmers, Rebecca Wests and Osvald Alvings of his plays undoubtedly represent. George Bernard Shaw, who championed Ibsen's drama, was sensitive to the politically negative impact of Darwin's thought on his writings, and in *The Quintessence of Ibsenism* Shaw tried to dismiss the impact of Darwinism on his favourite radical playwright by arguing that the appeal of Darwin for Ibsen was, straightforwardly, 'the mortal blow it dealt to the current travesties of Christianity'.[15] Whilst Ibsen's contempt for organized Christianity is writ large in his plays (not least in *Ghosts*, where he contemptuously satirizes Pastor Manders's time-serving conventionality), he was not a Darwinist merely for the iconoclastic clout of this most 'modern' of doctrines. His plays are far more *troubled* by Darwinism and specifically by the fin-de-siècle variant of Social Darwinism, degeneration theory, than Shaw was willing to concede. Max Nordau, a writer and contemporary of Ibsen who loathed the Norwegian's plays, was more alert to the influence of heredity theory in the drama than was Shaw, remarking scathingly that 'Heredity is [Ibsen's] hobby-horse, which he mounts in every one of his pieces. There is not a single trait in his personages, a single peculiarity of character, a single disease, that he does not trace to heredity.'[16] Nordau claimed that Ibsen had read Prosper Lucas's treatise on the first principles of heredity, written in 1847;[17] Ibsen's biographer, Michael Meyer, has remarked that in a general way heredity theory was much discussed by the Scandinavian community in Rome whilst Ibsen lived there, and points out that J. P. Jacobsen had translated Darwin's *Origin of Species* and *The Descent of Man* into Danish whilst in Rome, and it was quite possible that Ibsen would have had access to this.[18]

Ibsen's troubled negotiation of Social Darwinism and its fin-de-siècle offshoot, heredity theory, is clearly articulated in *Ghosts*. In the late nineteenth century there was a much expressed fear that biological and by extension social evolution did not always equate with racial and social improvement; there was a widespread recognition that the underbelly of evolutionary progress was racial degeneration. In *Ghosts*, the artistic, bohemian young Osvald Alving who tries to escape a narrow, bourgeois provincial life in Norway by living amongst artists and freethinkers in Paris, is forced to return to his homeland when he discovers he has syphilis. Paris was frequently figured, in late-Victorian literature, as the sexual 'other' city, the sexually risqué home of French decadence. One of the ironies at the heart of *Ghosts*, though, is that Osvald's contagion derives not from Paris but from his ostensibly 'respectable' married father, who was a chamberlain to boot. This, the play suggests, is where the real canker, the real cultural degeneration is located: not in the sexually exciting Parisian metropolis where Osvald's artist friends don't bother to get married, but in the respectable bourgeois fjordlands outside Bergen in Norway. It was presumably this which upset the reviewers of *Ghosts*. And they really were very upset. *Ghosts*' London première was put on by the newly formed Independent Theatre Society in 1891, ten years after it was written. It only survived one performance, and the outpouring of critical venom it aroused has scarcely been equalled in theatre history. Over five hundred articles appeared on the subject of the play and in one of the most vituperative of them it was famously described as 'An open drain; a loathsome sore unbandaged; a dirty act done publicly'.[19] The establishment's vehement critical reaction substantiates the play's radically subversive status, but such a status is nonetheless undermined by the fact that Osvald Alving returns to the prison of the bourgeois family to die defeated. Many of Ibsen's plays deal with young people's attempts to break with the past and with tradition, and many of them fail. Osvald's failure has rather more to do with biological inheritance than with social oppression, even though the former clearly serves in the play as a metaphor for the latter. Osvald inherits syphilis from his dissolute father, and also inherits his alcoholism and his predisposition to make sexual advances to dependent social inferiors. In a comparable way Regina, the illegitimate daughter of Captain Alving, appears to have inherited her mother's weakness for such sexual advances, and her future at the close of the play, with the offer of what seems to amount to 'hostess' work at a home for retired seamen, is arguably as determined as Osvald Alving's descent into paralysis. At the fin de siècle, the Darwinian theory of evolution, which at the mid-century had manifested itself, to freethinkers at least, as a theory of progress, had degenerated into a theory of inheritance with socially deterministic, politically stifling results.

The influence of hereditary theory on *Ghosts* is intricately bound up with its status as *naturalist* drama. For the realism of *Ghosts* is of that extreme kind which emphasizes the physical basis of human life, the ways in which our social relations are rooted in biology. The school of literary naturalism to which Ibsen's *Ghosts* belongs (despite Ibsen's protestations to the contrary) is strongly associated with the novels of Emile Zola, and it was mainly at Zola's prompting that *Ghosts* was first staged in France in 1890.

If *Ghosts* is a self-consciously 'new' naturalistic form of theatre, it none the less retains some traditional dramatic qualities, such as the Aristotelian unities: the entire action takes place during the course of twenty-four hours, and there is a single location for the play. This is, probably, Ibsen's most economically constructed play. Apart from one or two lengthy expostulations on the part of Manders, there is very little dramatic 'slack' in this sharply focused drama. The sharply focused pain and suffering of the main protagonists, and the terribly determined nature of their lives, brings to mind the Greek tragedies of Aeschylus and Sophocles. The difference is that Ibsen is concerned not with historic figures from a mythical past, but with living and breathing recognizable citizens of nineteenth-century Norway. *Ghosts* was the first great tragedy to have been written about ostensibly unheroic, unexceptional middle-class people who speak in plain, idiomatic prose. The tragedy is shocking, but the dramatic action itself is not melodramatic. The most dreadful human suffering is lived out every day in the most ordinary of living rooms – this is Ibsen's central observation in *Ghosts*, and it is for this that it is quintessentially a 'modern' tragedy.

Ibsen himself was acutely conscious of the ways in which *Ghosts* broke through the dominant moral and aesthetic codes of his day. In a letter to Otto Borchsenius, 28 January 1882, the playwright conceded that:

> It may well be that in certain respects this play is somewhat audacious. But I thought the time had come when a few boundary marks had to be shifted. And it was much easier for me, as an elder writer, to do this than for the many younger writers who might want to do something of the kind. I was prepared for a storm to break over me... What has most depressed me has been not the attacks themselves, but the lack of guts which has been revealed in the ranks of the so-called liberals in Norway. They are poor stuff with which to man the barricades.[20]

Ibsen had been horribly disappointed that the liberal newspapers and cultural commentators in Norway had not supported him over the controversy aroused by *Ghosts*. He had hoped for more from these influential organs in the formulation of public opinion. But it seems that a fear of 'public opinion' had silenced Ibsen's sometime journalistic supporters. Pastor Manders is adamant, in *Ghosts*, that 'we have no right to antagonise public opinion' (*GI*, 41), and it was such moral pusillanimity that Ibsen was to attack with astonishing ferocity in his next play, *An Enemy of the People*.

3

Liberalism and its Discontents: Ibsen's Politics in *An Enemy of the People*

'Ibsenism' and Ibsen are not synonymous. Whilst George Bernard Shaw, Eleanor Marx and other Ibsenites in late-Victorian London hailed the Norwegian playwright as honorary spokesperson for their various socialistic causes, Ibsen himself was politically uncommitted, never joining any political party or supporting unequivocally a particular political faction. As Michael Meyer has wryly noted, the one political demonstration in which the Norwegian took part involved the defiant cheering of an elderly German, Havro Harring, who was deported from Christiania in May 1850 for writing a radical play. Living in Italy in 1867, the strongest feeling provoked in Ibsen by Garibaldi's invasion of Rome was a sense of irritation that the trains were no longer running on time.[1] Never a sectarian in politics, he was, in his plays, essentially a liberal individualist, with Nora Helmer as his dramatic archetype (and this partly explains his appeal to late-Victorian feminism, which was very much a product of nineteenth-century Liberalism). Despite his often-cited speech to a workers' procession in Trondheim on 14 June 1885, in which he had predicted that 'The transformation of social conditions which is now being undertaken in the rest of Europe is very largely concerned with the future status of the workers and of women', it is I think difficult to appropriate Ibsen's work for socialism in quite the way the Shavian Ibsenites of the 1880s and 1890s did. Ibsen was very much of the avant-garde in as much as that he wished to disrupt and overturn the social, political and aesthetic status quo and to enable the birth of a new order of things. But his was a completely non-aligned avant-gardism which cannot readily be identified with either the political 'left' or the political 'right'. Whilst in *The Pillars of Society* (1877), for example, the object of attack is an extreme right-wing figure, in *An Enemy of the People* (1882) Ibsen turns on those mealy-mouthed liberals who had joined in the general condemnation of his naturalist play, *Ghosts* (1881), in the previous year.

The savage satire of *An Enemy of the People* is directed against the moral timidity – as Ibsen saw it – of the supposedly 'progressive' liberal press in Norway. In a letter to Georg Brandes, written in 1882 in advance of the publication of his play, Ibsen refers to the newspaper men's lack of courage:

> What is one to say of the attitude taken by the so-called liberal press? These leaders who talk and write of freedom and progress, and at the same time allow themselves to be the slaves of the supposed opinions of their subscribers? I become more and more convinced that there is something demoralising about involving oneself in politics and attaching oneself to a party. Under no circumstances will I ever link myself with any party which has the majority behind it. Björnson says: 'The majority is always right'. As a practising politician I suppose he has to say that. But I say: 'The minority is always right'. I am of course not thinking of the minority of reactionaries who have been left astern by the big central party which we call liberal; I mean the minority which forges ahead in territory which the majority has not yet reached. I believe that he is right who is most closely attuned to the future.... In the course of their undeniably worthy efforts to turn our country into a democratic community, people have unwittingly gone a good way towards turning us into a mob community.[2]

It is this process – a shift from democratic liberalism to mob rule – that Ibsen articulates in *An Enemy of the People*, and his own political sentiments as articulated in this letter to Brandes are almost identical to those of his main protagonist, Dr Stockmann. When handing the play over to his publisher, Ibsen noted with humour that: 'It has been fun working on the play ... Dr Stockmann and I got on most excellently; we agree about so many things; but the Doctor has a more muddled head on his shoulders than I have'.[3]

In this play from 1882, Dr Stockmann, the public health officer in a small Norwegian spa town, discovers that the town's water supply has been contaminated by typhus because, in a cost-cutting exercise, the town council, led by his own brother, hasn't laid the water mains deeply enough. Stockmann expects the local leaders – property owners, journalists and tradesmen – to support his determination to publicize the health threat, and initially they do. But as soon as they realize that they will have to pay extra taxes in order for the water mains to be relaid, they turn against the doctor and denounce him as an enemy of the people, bent on destroying the town's source of income (the new, elegant spa baths), as well as its reputation. The lumpen proletariat of the town – this is how Ibsen characterizes them – are easily persuaded to turn against Stockmann: they stone his house and try to drive him out of the town. Stockmann rounds on them, and in a series of impassioned tirades which dominate most of the play's fourth act, he condemns the mass of the people as an ignorant mob, bestial and sheep-like. 'This is the discovery I've made today!' he tells a public meeting:

> The most dangerous enemies of truth and freedom are the majority!... The majority is never right! Never, I tell you! That's one of those community lies that free, thinking men have got to rebel against! Who form the majority – in any country? The wise, or the fools? I think we'd all have to agree that the fools are in a terrifying, overwhelming majority all over the world! But in the name of God it can't be right that the fools should rule the wise!... The ones who are right are a few isolated individuals like me! The minority is always right!... My whole point is precisely this, that it's the masses, the mob, this damned majority – they're the thing that's poisoning the sources of our spiritual life and contaminating the ground we walk on!... Think first of a simple mongrel – one of those filthy, ragged, common curs that lope along the streets and defile the walls of our houses. And then put that mongrel next to a greyhound with a distinguished pedigree whose ancestors have been fed delicate meals for generations and have had the opportunity to listen to harmonious voices and music. Don't you think the brain of that greyhound is differently developed from that of the mongrel? (*EPIV*, 192–5)

And so he goes on, in a similar vein, for the rest of the act.

Although it is the sheep-like ignorance of the masses which Ibsen appears most to fear, he puts the blame for their ignorance squarely on the shoulders of those members of the liberal bourgeoisie who choose to misinform them – the journalists and editors of the town's 'radical' newspaper. Stockmann is a regular contributor to the *People's Tribune*. As Hovstad, the editor, remarks: 'Yes, he usually drops us a line when he thinks the truth needs to be told about something' (*EPI*, 124). Stockmann has an abstract, absolute conception of truth and a firm belief that freedom of speech is every individual's right, whatever the wishes or needs of the majority. He expects the press in a liberal and democratic society to be free and independent, uncompromised by capital interests. This classic liberal view is, though, shown to be at odds with capital interests: the newspaper editor is unwilling to tell the truth if to do so will damage his and others' interests. Hovstad and Billing, dependent as they are on the capital of Aslaksen (the printer) in order to run their newspaper, and having to cater for the interests and concerns of a mass public, quickly recognize and accept that their newspapers are nothing but the mouthpieces of particular interests, in which they have a personal investment (their livelihoods) despite their liberal leanings. Freedom of speech is one of the main tenets of modern liberal democracy, and yet it is a tenet which can be thoroughly at odds with those capital interests on which liberal democracies are founded. Such a conflict is given a classic expression in the play in an exchange between Stockmann and his brother, the Mayor:

> MAYOR: But as a subordinate official at the Baths you have no right to express any opinion which conflicts with that of your superiors . . .
> DR STOCKMANN: I must be free to say what I think about anything!
>
> (*EPII*, 155)

An Enemy of the People sharply articulates a classic liberal dilemma: how to harmonize individual freedoms and concerns with the interests of the wider community. Raymond Williams has articulated with great lucidity the liberal predicament that underpins so many of Ibsen's plays:

> We have to push past Ibsen's undoubted social consciousness to discover, at its roots, [an] individual consciousness. Certainly there is to be reform, the 'sick earth' is to be 'made whole', but this is to happen, always, by an individual act in the liberal conscience, *against* society. Change is never to be *with* people; if others come, they can at most be led. But also change, significantly often, is against people, it is against their wills that the liberator is thrown, and disillusion is then rapid.[4]

Dr Stockmann wishes to 'heal' the town, the decontamination of the water supply acting as a metaphor for implicitly wider social reforms (Stockmann has a number of impoverished patients, whom he treats without payment, and who clearly don't benefit from the political and institutional status quo). He initially values public support, welcoming the backing of the majority; but as soon as his eyes are opened to the moral limitations of this majority his disillusionment is total. It is at this point that his project of liberation turns into a campaign for change *against* society.

Dr Stockmann takes an extreme liberal-individualist position, determined to exercise his right to free speech, his right to publicize the truth, no matter what the consequences are for the wider community. He is at once a libertarian, an individualist and, significantly, anti-democratic, eventually campaigning for an aristocracy of the intellect. He maintains that the rights of the individual and abstract concepts of liberty and truth are more important than owning and defending property, earning a fortune and taking care of the interests of one's own family, all of which were central preoccupations of nineteenth-century bourgeois liberalism. When Stockmann speaks out against the liberal attitudes of men such as Hovstad, in the final act, he is attacking a pragmatic, modified kind of liberalism which is willing to compromise and to form an alliance with the existing ruling forces.[5] Ibsen is sympathetic towards Stockmann's position which, however, is shown to be untenable. Stockmann believes that with truth on his side he is powerful; but the play shows that money and economic clout, rather than 'truth' and moral rectitude, produce power. Stockmann's tragedy is that he is ignorant of the forces he is up against. Right from the beginning of the play he is shown to be an innocent as far as money and economics are concerned: he spends more than he earns, freely invites friends and colleagues to dinner, and naïvely believes that the 'Baths Committee' will raise his salary in recognition of the importance of his report concerning the contamination of the town's water supply (they sack him instead!).

In the context of the play's action, Doctor Stockmann is morally in the right concerning the town's sewers – the public health of the community should not be put at risk in order to protect the taxpayer's pocket. But the contaminating sewers, the cesspit on which, it is discovered, the spa town is built, acts in the play as a metaphor for *all* civil and political institutions. In his valorization of Dr Stockmann, Ibsen reacts against the petty politics of town councils, and against the political power of petty capitalist tradesmen. But he attacks at the same time the democratic process itself, and sets himself against the 'people', whom he represents as an undifferentiated mass – a classic nineteenth-century 'mob'. It is for his attack on the local politicians and corrupt capitalists that even this play has been beloved by political radicals, who have delighted in the travesty of an 'open' public meeting, at which Stockmann is prevented from telling the truth about the water supply and at which a 'free' vote is taken to silence him. Stanislavsky, who played the role of Dr Stockmann at the Moscow Arts Theatre in 1905, wrote of *An Enemy of the People* that it 'became the favourite play of the revolutionists'. In his autobiography, *My Life and Art*, Stanislavsky described a performance of the play which took place on the day of an anti-revolutionary massacre in Kasansky Square. At the moment when Dr Stockmann insists, in Act IV, on the 'fight for freedom and truth', the 'words aroused such pandemonium [in the theatre]', Stanislavsky writes, 'that it was necessary to stop the performance. The entire audience rose from its seats and threw itself towards the footlights . . . I saw hundreds of hands stretched towards me, all of which I was forced to shake.'[6]

Notwithstanding the revolutionists' enthusiasm, Stockmann's contempt for the masses, for the common people and for the democratic process itself, reveals a dimension of Ibsen's own politics – such as they were – that is not widely broadcast. Worshipped as Ibsen was by London's socialist intelligentsia at the end of the last century, it is curious to have Dr Stockmann's anti-collectivist, anti-democratic stance so ringingly endorsed by his Norwegian creator. Eleanor Marx, who first translated *An Enemy of the People* into English (then translated as *An Enemy of Society*), disliked the play and thought it unfortunate that it was included in the first printed selection of Ibsen's works in English. One can well imagine that Stockmann's anti-democratic libertarianism would jar with the communitarian, working-class orientation of Eleanor Marx's socialism. This same libertarianism and suspicion of the majority has, though, something in common with John Stuart Mill's political philosophy as articulated in his essay from 1869, *On Liberty*, in which he expresses the fear that the spread of the franchise could lead to a tyranny of the majority, and a morally dubious relegation of the rights and interests of the individual. Ibsen's distaste for the majority and his suspicion of any kind of social consensus is, though, extreme, and goes far beyond Mill's more measured defence of individual freedom in *On Liberty*.

Max Nordau, the reactionary fin-de-siècle cultural commentator and prophet of doom, described Ibsen dismissively as an 'egomaniacal anarchist'.[7] A bitter opponent of Ibsen, Nordau nonetheless does capture in this unflattering description something of the Norwegian's political temperament. Amongst the proliferating socialist parties of late-Victorian London, where Ibsen's work was so influential, was a body of anarchists, initially aligned to socialism through William Morris's Socialist League, but breaking away from it in 1888. An incipiently anarchistic political current does seem to run through Ibsen's play and emerges most interestingly at the close. Ostracized by the townspeople and refused employment, Dr Stockmann proposes to set up a free school for 'street urchins – real guttersnipes – mongrels . . . They have good heads on them sometimes.' (*EPV*, 221). He aims to educate his pupils as a new radical force, as free, liberated individuals and, despite his (and Ibsen's) ostensible contempt for the lowest echelons of society, there is a recognition here – shared by London's late-Victorian socialists – that a 'new' radical politics will emerge from the most oppressed social groups. At the same time, as far as Stockmann is concerned, the new politics will sweep away all existing political institutions: once he has educated his 'guttersnipes' he will get them to 'chase all these damned politicians into the Atlantic Ocean!' (*EPV*, 222). The insistence on untrammelled individual freedom and the refusal to countenance existing political institutions and processes does, it would seem, have something in common with anarchism's political project at the turn of the century.

Dr Stockmann's final utterance in *An Enemy of the People* is: 'The fact is, you see, that the strongest man in the world is he who stands most alone' (*EPV*, 222). The fact is, though, that he doesn't stand alone. Firmly beside him, throughout the play's action, is his daughter Petra, whose sexual independence, advanced political thinking and refusal to countenance political corruption or compromise mean that she is one of the most radical of Ibsen's female protagonists. It is Ibsen's women who will form the focus of the next chapter.

4

Ibsen's Women: *The Lady from the Sea, Hedda Gabler* and *Little Eyolf*

> Ibsen's knowledge of humanity is nowhere more obvious than in his portrayal of women. He amazes me by his painful introspection; he seems to know them better than they know themselves. (James Joyce, 'Ibsen's New Drama', 1900)[1]

> More than any other modern writer he has proved himself a prophet and an apostle of the cause of woman, no other modern writer has shown more sympathetic comprehension of her nature and its latent powers. (Louie Bennett, 'Ibsen as a Pioneer of the Woman Movement', 1910)[2]

From the moment that Ibsen's plays began to be translated and performed in Western Europe in the late nineteenth and early twentieth century, he began to receive remarkable accolades for his dramatic representation of women and womanhood. The extent of his personal sympathies for late-nineteenth-century feminism is rather ambivalent. Whilst in the notes he made for *A Doll's House,* for example, he reflected that 'A woman cannot be herself in contemporary society, it is an exclusively male society with laws drafted by men, and with counsel and judges who judge feminine conduct from a male point of view',[3] in a speech he made at a banquet given in his honour by the Norwegian Women's Rights League on 26 May 1898 he notoriously disavowed the apparent feminism of his dramas:

> I am not a member of the Women's Rights League. Whatever I have written has been without any conscious thought of making propaganda. I have been more poet and less social philosopher than people generally seem inclined to believe. I thank you for the

> toast, but must disclaim the honour of having consciously worked for the women's rights movement. I am not even quite clear as to just what this women's rights movement really is. To me it has seemed a problem of humanity in general.

The 'problem of humanity in general' to which Ibsen refers is his preoccupation with the obstacles put in the way of individual liberty and freedom by bourgeois society in the late nineteenth century. It was Ibsen's commitment to individual freedom which appealed to nineteenth-century liberal feminism in Scandinavia and Western Europe, for it was on this that the Women's Movement based its claims for women's independence. So that although Ibsen tended to believe in a relatively abstract concept of the freedom of the individual, his dramatic quest for such freedom happened to coincide with the demands of a radical counter-culture in late-Victorian Britain as well as comparable radical movements in Norway and Sweden.

Ibsen does appear to have a number of feminist credentials in biographical terms. In 1884 he supported a petition in favour of separate property rights for married women, and was on confidential terms with Camilla Collett, Norway's best-known feminist in the nineteenth century. He and Collett had intensively debated marriage and women's place in society in the 1870s, and he acknowledged without reserve the considerable influence she had on his writing.[4] Ibsen chose as his lifelong partner Suzannah Thoresen, who, widely read in literature and drama and with 'advanced' social views, was a distinctly 'modern' woman, what we would now call a feminist. She married Ibsen in 1858.[5] Ibsen also sympathetically represents distinctly 'emancipated' women in his plays: Lona Hessel in *The Pillars of Society*, Petra Stockmann in *An Enemy of the People*, and Hilde Wangel in *The Master Builder*, for example. Both Lona Hessel and Hilde Wangel dress in a decidedly unladylike fashion, with Hessel cutting her hair short and wearing men's boots, and Wangel marching on stage with her skirt hitched up and carrying a rucksack. Such 'masculine' attire would have struck a chord with the feminist Rational Dress campaign in late-Victorian Britain, which rejected the physically confining clothes deemed suitable for 'respectable' women. A number of Ibsen's women are well educated, too (Rebecca West, in *Rosmersholm*, and Petra Stockmann, for example), or at least have a strong desire to be educated (Nora Helmer in *A Doll's House* and Bolette Wangel in *The Lady from the Sea*). One of the major projects of the nineteenth-century women's movement was to improve educational opportunity for women, and Ibsen clearly demonstrated sympathy for women's educational ambition in his plays.

It would be wrong, though, to try to claim Ibsen for a polemical canon of distinctly feminist literature, for his plays characteristically diagnose women's ills rather than propose cures, and there are few feminist victories in his drama. The interest of his plays in relation to nineteenth-century womanhood is their painful dissection of the constrictive nature of women's experience in contemporary society, and the psychological and emotional damage such experience has on them. Arguably the most interesting roles for female actresses, and the most searching interrogations of what it was like to be a woman in the bourgeois backwaters of nineteenth-century Norway, are to be found in plays where women are defeated, despairing or resigned to the disappointments and imperfections of a nineteenth-century woman's life. Feminist or not, many an actress has memorably recreated Ibsen's heroines. Elizabeth Robins, the great fin-de-siècle American actress, remarked that 'no dramatist has ever meant so much to the women of the stage as Henrik Ibsen',[6] and many impressive performances have been turned in, in the second half of the twentieth century, by actresses of distinction such as Janet McTeer, Juliet Stevenson, Diana Rigg, Glenda Jackson and Susannah York.

Ibsen's interest in individual liberty and freedom, which guaranteed his appeal to Victorian feminism, also affiliates him with political liberalism. The limitations of liberalism in terms of its analysis of social class can interestingly be traced in Ibsen's great plays for women actresses, inasmuch as that his leading female protagonists are always specifically *bourgeois* women, with working-class women figuring as semi-invisible maidservants whose need for freedom and liberty is, presumably, of no interest to Ibsen's projected audiences. Anne-Marie, the maidservant in *A Doll's House*, has, we learn in passing, had to give up a child in order to care for Nora when she was a girl. As an adult, the infantilized, decorous Nora, naughtily munching macaroons, needs the marginalized maidservant to oil the cogs of her bourgeois domestic world. Nor, presumably, will the need for Anne-Marie's services disappear once Nora has renounced her domestic life; the maidservant will presumably be left 'holding the baby', so to speak, when Nora leaves the marital home and her children in a quest for freedom and her 'self'. Anne-Marie's marginalization (and that of others like her – Bertha, for example, in *Hedda Gabler*) reveals the limitations of a liberal individualism which Victorian feminists eagerly embraced and which Ibsen appears soundly to endorse in his plays.

The class-specific nature of Ibsen's interest in individual freedom and liberty does not mean his plays lack an analysis of the economic basis of the bourgeois domesticity he so savagely satirizes. Nowhere is his attack on the bourgeois social economy more powerfully displayed than in his dramatic account of the cash-nexus upon which late-nineteenth century bourgeois marriage is built. Nora, in *A Doll's House*, characterizes herself as an object of exchange between her father and her husband (see chapter 1), and Ellida Wangel, in *The Lady from the Sea*, regards her marriage contract in much the same light. As she and her husband, Dr Wangel, contemplate their now sexless marriage, she reflects bitterly that when Wangel had proposed to her:

> I – I stood there, helpless, so completely alone. So when you came and offered to – support me for life, I – agreed....But I shouldn't have accepted. I shouldn't have sold myself, not at any price....I didn't come to your home of my own free will. (*LS*IV, 187)

For a while the only way out of their marital misery seems to be divorce – a process Ellida describes as 'Cancel[ling] the bargain' (*LS*IV, 188). Ellida's stepdaughter, Bolette, compromises herself in precisely the same way when she halfheartedly accepts a proposal of marriage from Arnolm, her old schoolmaster, whom she does not love, on the basis that she will no longer 'have to worry about the future. Not to have to pinch and scrape – ' (*LS*V, 200). And Hedda Gabler, at 29, is driven by her own complicity with bourgeois social conventions to marry the well-meaning but idiotic George Tesman, to whom she is brutally open about the economic basis of her choice of marriage partner: 'You agreed that we should enter society. And keep open house. That was the bargain.' It is when she realizes that they will not be able to afford 'to have a liveried footman' nor 'the bay mare you promised me' that Hedda begins to despair of her marriage (*HG*I, 271–2). In *Little Eyolf* the situation is reversed. Alfred Allmers, we learn, married his wife Rita mainly for her wealth – for 'your "gold and your green forests"' (*LE*I, 239), as he so delicately puts it. In his desire to take care of his half-sister, Asta (to whom, it later transpires, he is unrelated), Allmers is willing to sell himself into a marriage with a woman he fears. Allmers's fear of Rita is explicit:

> ALLMERS: My first feeling for you was not love, Rita.
> RITA: What was it, then?
> ALLMERS: Fear.
>
> (*LE*II, 267)

It is Rita's passionate sexuality that frightens Allmers, and it is interesting that it is Ibsen's wealthiest female protagonist, who can afford to marry for love rather than for the accoutrements of bourgeois domesticity, who is the most openly sexual and sensuous. Rita's sexuality is pronounced. Her husband hesitantly acknowledges this in his recognition of the particular quality of her beauty: 'You were so – so consumingly beautiful, Rita – ' (*LE*II, 267), and she herself makes no secret of her sexual needs throughout the play:

> RITA: . . . I only want you! Nothing else, in the whole world! (*throws herself again around his neck*) I want you, you, you!
> ALLMERS: Let me go! You're strangling me!
>
> (*LE*I, 24)

As they painfully dissect the ruins of their now-celibate marriage (Allmers has been impotent since their child was crippled, falling off a table, unsupervised, as Rita and he made love), Rita herself acknowledges her sexual needs: 'I am flesh and blood! I cannot drowse my life away like a fish! To be walled up . . . With a man who is no longer mine, mine, mine!' (*LE*II, 267)

Ibsen's dramatic expression of female sexuality goes far beyond what most writers of the period would have dared to represent. Although in the Decadent literature of the period women are frequently figured as femmes fatales or sexual vamps, such representations only offer negative accounts of women's sexuality. Women's sexual desire in Ibsen's plays is treated with far more insight than is the case in most other textual productions of the period.[7] Ellida Wangel's sexuality, in *The Lady from the Sea*, is expressed symbolically through the myth of the mermaid who, now married to the land, pines away, longing for the sea. The sea in the play is associated with freedom and sexuality, a sexuality with a dangerous edge to it given its association with the murderous sailor who tries to lure Ellida away from her marriage to Dr Wangel. Ellida describes the 'Stranger' (the sailor) as 'demonic', as 'something that appals – and attracts' (*LS*IV, 189), and his hold over her is clearly sexual. As a young girl she agreed to a symbolic 'sea-marriage' with him, the bond forged by tying their two rings together and throwing them into the ocean. In trying to explain to her husband the Stranger's attractions, Ellida inchoately describes the 'horrible, unfathomable power he has over my mind.' *(LSII, 158)*

An early reviewer scoffingly described Ellida's attraction to the Stranger as a symptom of her crazily disordered mind: 'We have the crazy woman all over again, only crazier than ever'.[8] Women's sexuality has – when recognized at all – often been regarded in Western cultures as a symptom of madness or, to use Freud's clinical terminology, hysteria. Hedda Gabler's 'crazy' preoccupation with her dead father's pistols – she twice threatens sexually predatory men with them, lends one to a spurned lover, urging him to commit suicide, and finally shoots herself in the head – dramatically represents both her own frustrated sexuality, stifled as it is in a conventional marriage to a man with the sex appeal of an overweight puppy-dog, and a desire to escape her femininity altogether; the Freudian symbolism of the pistols too obvious to require commentary. Hedda's sexuality is complex. Described in the stage directions as having 'steel-grey' eyes 'with an expression of cold, calm serenity' (*HG*I, 252), she is shown clearly to be repressing her real feelings for most of the play's length, and this greatly increases the dramatic tension. We learn that as a young woman she used to wring from Loevborg details of his erotic, licentious life, because as a young girl she wanted 'to be allowed a glimpse into a forbidden world of whose existence she is supposed to be ignorant' (*HG*I, 292). And yet, we are informed, as soon as Loevborg proposed a sexual relationship with her, on the night of these erotic revelations, she reacted violently against him, threatening him with her father's pistol, refusing her lover's advances on the basis that 'I was afraid. Of the scandal' (*HG*II, 292). Hedda, finally, is a victim of her own conventionality, preferring to die than openly to flout social codes. But her denial of her sexuality leads to violence and trauma. Her very real and often dangerous passions erupt at certain points in the drama, notably when Judge Brack visits her, a pillar of the community whose ambition is to subject her to him sexually in an adulterous relationship. She shoots a pistol at him, and it is never clear whether or not the 'miss' is intentional. The threat she poses to the self-satisfied bourgeois world in which she lives is also made apparent in her response to Thea Elvsted, whom she affects to welcome at the same time as burning with resentment at her rival's success with Loevborg, whom she regards as her own. 'I think I'll burn off your hair after all', she threatens – and it would be a brave director who would ask an actress to pronounce this in the tones of a harmless joke (*HG*II, 299). The most telling outbreaks of violence are triggered by any reference to the pregnancy which Hedda denies, even to herself, for much of the play's length. The well-meaning maiden aunt Juliana, who wants nothing better than a nest of babies to attend to, fails to spot the great irritation she produces in Hedda every time she refers to a possible pregnancy, and when George Tesman himself ponders the possibility – 'Hasn't she filled out?' as he oafishly puts it to Judge Brack – Hedda tersely silences him: 'Oh, do stop it' (*HG*I, 267). With Judge Brack, she is more explicit:

> BRACK: . . . suppose you were to find yourself faced with what people call – to use the conventional phrase – the most solemn of human responsibilities? (*Smiles*) A new responsibility, little Mrs Hedda.
>
> HEDDA (angrily): Be quiet! Nothing like that's going to happen. . . . I've no leanings in that direction, Judge. I don't want any – responsibilities.
>
> (*HG*II, 282)

It is his dramatic presentation of women's complex and often tormented negotiation of motherhood which singles out Ibsen as one of the greatest delineators of women's lives in the late nineteenth century. Ibsen's mothers either abandon their children (Nora Helmer), farm them out for others to look after

(Mrs Alving), wish them dead (Rita Allmers) or kill them prenatally through an act of suicide (Hedda Gabler). Such unhappy experiences of motherhood had loud echoes in British novels of the period, with New Womanish heroines such as Sue Bridehead (in Hardy's *Jude the Obscure*, 1895), Evadne Frayling (in Sarah Grand's *The Heavenly Twins*, 1893), Lyndall (in Olive Schreiner's *The Story of an African Farm*, 1883), Hadria Fullerton (in Mona Caird's *The Daughters of Danaus*, 1894) and Herminia Barton (in Grant Allen's *The Woman Who Did*, 1895) all experiencing motherhood as a desperately negative phase of their lives. In Ibsen's preliminary notes for *Hedda Gabler*, he wrote of women that 'They aren't all created to be mothers',[9] a non-judgemental insight which cut right across contemporary expectations of middle-class women in particular. And Ibsen's plays are littered with illegitimate children, the unwelcome by-products of illicit sexual relationships: Regina in *Ghosts*, Gina's daughter Hedvig in *The Wild Duck*, and Asta Allmers in *Little Eyolf*. There is also large-scale infant mortality: Ellida's dead baby in *The Lady from the Sea*, the sacrificial suicide of Hedvig in *The Wild Duck*, the baby Hedda Gabler takes with her into oblivion, and the Solnesses' dead infant twins in *The Master Builder*. Motherhood, for the nineteenth-century bourgeoisie, was meant to be the acme of a woman's experience; in Ibsen's plays it is the defining experience of women's lives, but rarely fulfilling.

The repulsion Hedda feels towards her pregnancy has complex origins. Clearly her desire to avoid motherhood is partly to do with the aversion she feels towards the cosy bourgeois domesticity which would then enfold and stifle her. She can hardly bring herself to speak explicitly of the pregnancy even to her husband:

> Well, I suppose you'd better know. I'm going to have – (*Breaks off and says violently*) No, no – you'd better ask your aunt JuJu: she'd tell you . . . (*Clenches her hands in despair*). Oh it's destroying me, all this – it's destroying me!'
>
> (*HG*IV, 322)

Her denial of her pregnancy also seems to be bound up with a denial of her own fierce sexuality. She enjoys listening to the details of Loevborg's sex life, but threatens to shoot him when he wants to have sex with her; she shoots herself dead when she discovers that she has become a sexual pawn in Judge Brack's power game. One director, seemingly having picked up on Hedda's fierce sexual reticence, first presents her 'in a pre-textual scene prowling round the drawing room in darkness, possibly after sex with Tesman, in a state of sighing desperation.'[10]

Equally complex is Hedda's burning of Loevborg's manuscript. As she throws the pages of his new book into the fire, she whispers to herself:

> I'm burning your child Thea! You with your beautiful wavy hair! (*She throws a few more pages into the stove.*) The child Eilert Loevborg gave you. (*Throws the rest of the manuscript in.*) I'm burning it! I'm burning your child!
>
> (*HG*III, 317)

This is a complex act of vengeance, jealous regret, and displaced aggression against the child she herself so unwillingly carries. It is also, of course, a supremely dramatic moment in the play.

Rita Allmers's resentment of a maternal role is just as pronounced, and just as complex, in *Little Eyolf*. That the guilt-inducing presence of their crippled child has been a major factor in Allmers's sexual paralysis quickly becomes clear. Equally, Rita's continuing sexual needs are given full dramatic expression: her inability emotionally to fulfil herself through maternity distinguishes her sharply from traditional models of femininity in the nineteenth century, when motherhood was regarded as the emotional goal of all women, their sexuality awakened only in the interests of procreation. By contrast, Rita finds Little Eyolf's disruptive presence in their marital relationship a 'hateful' thing:

> ALLMERS: You call our child hateful?
> RITA (*violently*): I do! For what he has done to us!... this child is a living wall between us.... I wish to God I had never borne him.
> ALLMERS: Sometimes you almost frighten me, Rita.
> ...
> RITA: ... I can't be just a mother.... I won't, I tell you – I can't. I want to be everything to you. To you, Alfred.
> ALLMERS: But you are, Rita. Through our child –
>
> (*LE*I, 245–6)

Many literary texts in the late nineteenth century began to explore the burdens rather than the joys of motherhood, and in *Little Eyolf* the staring eyes of the dead child, drowned in the fjord, return to haunt Rita Allmers, racked as she is by guilt at her failure to love him:

> RITA: They say he lay on his back. With his eyes wide open.
> ALLMERS: With his eyes open? And quite still?
> RITA: Yes, quite still.... Day and night I shall see him lying there.
> ALLMERS: With his eyes wide open.
>
> (*LE*II, 261)

The lack of resistance displayed by the child as he plunges to his death resonates with the suicide of 'Little Father Time' in Hardy's last novel, *Jude the Obscure*, published in the same year as *Little Eyolf*. Both young boys have a curiously 'wise', somewhat withdrawn demeanour, serious beyond their years, and both their deaths symbolically represent the tortured experience that motherhood had become for some independent-minded women at the turn of the century. Rita comes to regard Eyolf's death as retribution for the love that she was unable to give him. But her lack of maternal feeling is not *simply* an inherent characteristic. As she confides to Allmers in her grief, she had from the start felt upstaged in her role as mother to Eyolf by Asta, Allmers's half-sister, whose presence in their marriage has clearly been powerful and undermining:

> I did want him. But someone stood between us from the first.... His aunt.... Asta made him hers – right from the time it happened. The accident –
>
> (*LE*II, 262–3)

In the first act it is clear that Little Eyolf goes to Asta for reassurance rather than to his mother, shrinking close to her when the Rat-wife appears. Allmers, too, confides in Asta rather than Rita; it is only when both Asta and Eyolf have gone that Rita and Allmers really begin to communicate with one another.

Ellida Wangel's response to motherhood in *The Lady from the Sea* anticipates, but is more ambivalent than, Rita Allmers's tragic negotiation of the maternal role. Early in the play we learn that she and Wangel had a child who died in infancy, and that it was during her pregnancy that Ellida withdrew from a sexual relationship with her husband. Ellida also confides in Wangel that the dead child's eyes seemed to change colour whenever storms blew up in the fjord, and that – although clearly fathered by Wangel – he had the eyes of the Stranger, the sailor to whom

Ellida had once promised herself. Ellida's psychological disorder dates from her pregnancy, and it gradually emerges that the pregnancy and the subsequent death of her child have become linked in her mind to the infidelity she has shown towards the sailor, the man who first claimed her as his own. The child was not his, but should have been. In this play, as in *Little Eyolf*, maternity becomes associated with sexual guilt. In modern terms Ellida might be diagnosed as suffering from postnatal depression, a depression compounded by her unacknowledged grief (Wangel cannot even remember how old the infant was when it died). The loss of her child is exacerbated by the rejection Ellida feels she suffers at the hands of her step-daughters, Bolette and Hilde Wangel. She feels locked out of the Wangel family in much the same way as Rita feels she is rendered redundant by Asta in *Little Eyolf*. Right at the start of the play we witness the two girls celebrating their dead mother's birthday, and also learn that whilst Ellida spends her days in the summer in the garden, the two girls spend it on the veranda, with Wangel moving uneasily between his second wife and his daughters. Ellida feels that she lacks a role in the family. Deprived of her own child, she has nothing left but the erotic attraction to the Stranger, who wants her to be his alone:

> Don't you see? In this house I have nothing to keep me. I have no roots here, Wangel. The children are not mine. They don't love me. . . . I have been – outside – outside everything. From the first day I came here.
>
> (*LSV*, 194–5)

Interestingly in this regard, we never actually see Ellida *inside*, in the domestic sphere, throughout the whole play, which is mostly set in the garden, on the edge of domestic space, from which Ellida looks out longingly to the fjords, to the sea and to freedom. Wangel's initial response to Ellida's nervous depression, as doctor and husband, is to protect and incarcerate her in much the same way that the doctor-husband does in Charlotte Perkins Gilman's short story 'The Yellow Wallpaper', another text from the fin de siècle, published four years after *The Lady from the Sea*. But unlike the husband in Gilman's tale, Wangel does not insist on the notorious 'rest cure' for his wife, but instead gives her her freedom; the freedom to choose where she wants to live and with whom. That she freely decides to stay with him is anticipated in the play by Bolette's revelation that Hilde, the younger of the two girls, needs a mother:

ELLIDA (*half aloud to Bolette*): What's the matter with Hilde? She looks quite upset.
BOLETTE: Haven't you noticed what Hilde has been yearning for day after day?
ELLIDA: Yearning for?
BOLETTE: Ever since you entered this house.
ELLIDA: No, no. What!
BOLETTE: One single loving word from you.
ELLIDA: Ah! Could there be a place for me in this house? (*She clasps her hands to her head and stares ahead of her, motionless, as though torn by conflicting thoughts and emotions.*)

(*LSIV*, 192)

Both Ellida, at the end of this play, and Rita, at the end of *Little Eyolf*, take on the role of foster parent to children to whom biologically they are unrelated. It is only as foster parents that mothers are shown to have any chance of maternal fulfilment in Ibsen's plays. It is as if only when there is no biological or cultural coercion that 'motherhood' can bring emotional satisfaction to women. Aunt Juliana performs a comparable role in relation to George Tesman, in *Hedda Gabler*, as does Ella Rentheim in relation to Erhart Borkman in *John Gabriel Borkman*. And arguably Dr Stockmann, in *An Enemy of the People*, altruistically 'fosters' the street urchins whom he hopes to transform into a revolutionary force. A socialized view of parenting, divorced from the usual confines of the bourgeois nuclear family, seems to be more firmly endorsed in Ibsen's plays than traditional parental roles.

For Ellida Wangel and Rita Allmers, the fostering of others' children is an arguably weak alternative to the passionate sexual fulfilment that both women have desired and been denied. Whilst Ellida chooses this course of action of her 'own free will' (and it is for this reason that *The Lady from the Sea* is Ibsen's most optimistic play as far as the marriage relation is concerned), Rita's adoption of the village boys is a desperate act of expiation, an attempt to 'placate the eyes that stare at me', the accusing eyes of her dead child (*LE*III, 285). For both women, motherhood has brought more in the way of sorrow than of joy. Hedda

Gabler's plight is much worse. For her, maternity becomes implicated with a shabby, sexually dishonest life with a husband she despises. So grotesque a prospect does it become that she chooses to end her life rather than play the role of wife and mother to which she feels herself desperately unfitted.

5

Ibsen, Freud and Psychological Drama: *Rosmersholm* and *Peer Gynt*

In his 1909 study of obsessional neurosis, 'The Rat-Man', Freud recounts how this particular case had baffled him, seeming to resist all diagnosis, 'until one day', he writes, 'the Rat-Wife in Ibsen's *Little Eyolf* came up in the analysis, and it became impossible to escape the inference that in many of the shapes assumed by his obsessional deliria rats had another meaning still – namely, that of *children*'.[1] In *Little Eyolf*, the young, crippled child of Rita and Alfred Allmers is inexplicably lured to his death by the fairytale figure of the Rat-wife. Ostensibly inexplicable, his death can be understood in psychological terms as a fulfilment of Rita's desire to rid herself of the burden of motherhood. Psychologically it is *her* wish, never to have borne him, that strikes down the child. The Rat-wife's sinister question as she scuttles onto the stage – 'Begging your pardon – have your honours any troublesome thing that gnaws here in this house?... I'd be glad to rid you of it, if there was any gnawing thing that troubled you' (*LEI*, 233) – refers to the unwanted child's presence in the house. And yet Rita's reluctance as a mother is not straightforward. The repugnance she feels towards her son partly at least grows out of a sense of guilt that he fell and injured himself as an infant whilst she and Allmers were lovemaking. His crippled presence is now a constant reminder of that guilty act and of Alfred Allmers's subsequent sexual impotence. The psychological depth of *Little Eyolf* (1894), one of Ibsen's late plays, can be identified much earlier on in his dramatic output. The fact that Ibsen's middle and late plays tend to end with a discussion of a relationship, rather than with a denouement, is indicative of their psychological content. The tortured, painful conversation between Rita and Alfred Allmers at the close of *Little Eyolf*, for example, constitutes one of the most moving and memorable scenes in Ibsen's theatre. *A Doll's House* is an interestingly transitional play in this respect. For whilst a searching, relentless dissection of their failed marriage is insisted upon by Nora Helmer in the first 'serious talk' that she and her husband have ever had in eight years of marriage, right near the end of the play, what most audiences remember is the dramatic denouement, the slamming of the door. Nora Helmer is very much a realist character,[2] a socially representative 'type'. She is domestic woman, the Victorian angel in the house who finally casts her halo to the winds. By contrast, the much more difficult Hedda Gabler, who emanated from Ibsen's pen some eleven years later, is less a representative realist character than a psychological case study, the interest of *Hedda Gabler* inhering in the psychological motivation of Hedda's difficult and extreme behaviour. The same can be said of Rebecca West, the female lead in Ibsen's play from 1886, *Rosmersholm*.

Rosmersholm was the Ibsen play on which Freud commented most fully. The psychological content of the play also elicited rare praise from Strindberg, who generally had little positive to say about Ibsen's dramas. In an essay called 'Soul-Murder', Strindberg declared that *Rosmersholm* was 'unintelligible for the theatre public, mystical to the semi-educated, but crystal clear to anyone with a knowledge of modern psychology'.[3] Strindberg's assessment was correct. Following the play's London première in 1891, the theatre critic for *The Times* remarked caustically that 'a large number of the spectators went away in a state of some perplexity, conscious only of having witnessed the proceedings of a handful of disagreeable and somewhat enigmatical personages'.[4] And Clement Scott, the theatre critic for the *Daily Telegraph*, described *Rosmersholm* as:

> one of the strangest plays ever written...The old theory of playwriting was to make your story or your study as simple and direct as possible.... But Ibsen loves to mystify. He is as enigmatical as the sphinx....Up to this hour it would surely puzzle the most philosophical Ibsenite to say clearly and decisively why Rebecca West chose such a man as Rosmer for her helpmate and soul-companion,

> and having got him into her toils and Mrs Rosmer conveniently at the bottom of the pond in the garden, why she should refuse the marriage which it was her original object to obtain.[5]

To Scott's credit, Sigmund Freud asked of the play exactly the same question. Why, Freud demanded, does this courageous woman, who has had no qualms about Rosmer's former wife ever before, first show utter delight when Rosmer proposes marriage, and then, in the very next breath, threaten suicide?[6] But Freud, unlike Clement Scott and other contemporary theatregoers, had a ready answer to the question posed. It is to Freud's reading of the play that the following account is indebted.

In this play, as in so much of Ibsen's dramatic output, the past – in this case past crime – returns to haunt its perpetrators. In *Rosmersholm* the past is configured as a Freudian return of the repressed. We learn in the play's first act that prior to the action of the play John Rosmer's wife, Beata, has drowned herself in the mill-race, an act of despair attributed to an unstable, mentally diseased mind. Both before and after the suicide, Rebecca West has played the role of spiritual helpmeet to John Rosmer. Whilst there is no sex in the relationship, it emerges in the play's fourth and final act that both Rebecca and John Rosmer have desired each other sexually (and any production of the play should deliberately build up an atmosphere of powerful sexual tension between the two main protagonists), and that Rebecca helped drive Beata to suicide by pretending to her that she, Rebecca, was carrying Rosmer's child. The double suicide at the play's close could be attributed to the terrible sense of guilt they both feel surrounding Beata's death. But Freud was dissatisfied with this as a total explanation of Rebecca's actions. For even after she has confessed to Rosmer the heinous crime of driving his wife to suicide, Rosmer persists in his desire to marry her, proposing once more and so, by implication, forgiving her. After the second proposal, Freud observes, Rebecca:

> does not answer, as she should, that no forgiveness can rid her of the feeling of guilt she has incurred from her malignant deception of poor Beata; but she charges herself with another reproach which affects us as coming strangely from this free-thinking woman, and is far from deserving the importance which Rebecca attaches to it.... She has had sexual relations with another man; and we do not fail to observe that these relations, which occurred at a time

> when she was free and accountable to nobody, seem to her a greater hindrance to the union with Rosmer than her truly criminal behaviour to his wife.[7]

The 'reproach' to which Freud refers is described by Rebecca as follows: 'Before I came to Rosmersholm – something happened to me – ... Something more terrible –' (*R*IV, 102). Freud suggests that there are buried hints in the play that this 'something' is a sexual relationship with Dr West, whom she thought was her foster father but whom Kroll, at the start of the play's fourth act, reveals to her as her biological parent. The second 'reproach' Rebecca has to bear, then, is an act of incest. Freud's detection of buried hints that there has been a sexual relationship between Rebecca and Dr West before the play's action is astute. In the first act, Kroll, at this point ostensibly sympathetic, describes the now-dead Dr West as 'unreasonable ... once he got paralysed', and commiserates with Rebecca over the amount of care and attention she had been obliged to lavish on him. But Rebecca hesitatingly demurs: 'Oh, he wasn't so – unreasonable, in the old days' (*R*I, 35). It is in the pause – in Rebecca's hesitation in describing her relation to Dr West – that the buried hint lies. In Act II, Rebecca's response to Rosmer's lamentation over his sense of lost innocence following Kroll's critical attitude towards him in relation to his wife's death, is also telling:

> ROSMER (*shakes his head sadly*): I shall never conquer this – not completely. ... I shall never again be able to enjoy the one thing that makes life so wonderful to live.
> REBECCA (*over the back of the chair, more quietly*): What is that, John?
> ROSMER (*looks up at her*): The sense of calm and happy innocence.
> REBECCA (*takes a step back*): Yes. Innocence.
>
> (*R*II, 73)

A director would be well advised to emphasize Rebecca's 'step back' here, and to stress, too, the dramatic pause which is implied by her tersely articulated response to Rosmer: 'Yes. Innocence'. Such emphases would make it possible to suggest that Rebecca's own sense of lost innocence is based on rather more than her betrayal of Beata. That her sense of lost innocence and feelings of sexual guilt emanate from an incestuous relationship with Dr West becomes clearer in Act IV, when

Kroll maliciously reveals to her the likelihood that she is Dr West's daughter. As Kroll himself remarks, the extremity of her horror at such a revelation is rather surprising from such a free-thinking woman, given that her illegitimacy was in no way her own fault. The scene proceeds as follows:

> KROLL: Your mother's occupation must of course have brought her into frequent contact with the district physician.
> REBECCA: It did.
> KROLL: And as soon as your mother dies, he takes you into his own home. He treats you harshly. Yet you stay with him.... Put up with all his tantrums – look after him until the day he dies.... What you did for him I attribute to an unconscious filial instinct. Your whole conduct seems to me irrefutable evidence of your birth.
> REBECCA (*vehemently*): There isn't a word of truth in anything you say! ...
> REBECCA (*walks around, twisting and untwisting her hands*): It isn't possible. It's only something you're trying to make me imagine. It can't be true. It can't! Not possibly – !
> KROLL (*gets up*): But my dear – why in heaven's name are you taking it so to heart? You quite frighten me. What am I to imagine?
> REBECCA: Nothing. You are to imagine nothing.
>
> (*RIV*, 87–8)

The reason Rebecca is taking the revelation of her birth 'so to heart' is that she has been Dr West's lover, a possibility that Kroll is quick to pick up on – 'You quite frighten me. What am I to imagine?' – and which Rebecca confusedly semi-articulates in her later reflection that 'The Doctor had taught me so many things. Everything I knew about life – then –' (*RIV*, 91). That she has been Oedipally involved with her father explains, according to the Freudian model, her attraction to John Rosmer. Thirteen years her senior, of a traditional, patriarchal lineage, he too is a paternal figure whom she both nurtures and learns from. And just as, as soon as her mother died, she usurped her mother's role as Dr West's lover, so she ousts the wife in the Rosmer home, with the aim of replacing her in the husband's sexual affections. And, arguably, the reason Rebecca thinks John Rosmer needs no children – 'Pastor Rosmer wasn't made to sit here listening to little children crying' she tells Mrs Helseth, the housekeeper, in Act III – is because she wants to be everything to Rosmer, child, wife and lover.

According to Freud, the reason Rebecca threatens suicide when Rosmer proposes to her is that her unconscious knowledge, even before Kroll's revelation, that her relationship with Dr West was incestuous, suddenly rushes to the surface. This is the 'something more terrible' she tentatively describes to Rosmer towards the play's close. In Rosmer's proposal she recognizes the Oedipal pattern which has shaped her young sexual life and she recoils from it with horror. But she has been subconsciously aware of the status of her sexual relationship with Dr West all along. As the tidal wave of sexual guilt and self-reproach has gradually built up in relation to Beata's suicide, Rebecca's supposed foster father has very gradually revealed himself in her sexual consciousness as her biological father. Recognizing in Rosmer another father figure, old incest fears are reawakened and she becomes sexually paralysed and suicidal. Freud himself describes the incest taboo which shapes the dramatic action of Ibsen's most densely psychological play as follows:

> Rebecca's feeling of guilt has its source in the reproach of incest, even before Kroll, with analytical perspicacity, has made her conscious of it. If we reconstruct her past, expanding and filling in the author's hints, we may feel sure that she cannot have been without some inkling of the intimate relationship between her mother and Dr West. It must have made a great impression on her when she became her mother's successor with this man. She stood under the domination of the Oedipus complex, even though she did not know that this universal phantasy had in her case become a reality. When she came to Rosmersholm, the inner force of this first experience drove her into bringing about, by vigorous action, the same situation which had been realised in the original instance through no doing of hers – into getting rid of the wife and mother, so that she might take her place with the husband and father. She describes with a convincing insistence how, against her will, she was obliged to proceed, step by step, to the removal of Beata.... Everything that happened to her at Rosmersholm, her falling in love with Rosmer and her hostility to his wife, was from the first a consequence of the Oedipus complex – an inevitable replica of her relations with her mother and Dr West.[8]

Rebecca West, who baffled *Rosmersholm*'s earliest critics, is a fascinating study in feminine sexual psychology. No less interesting, though, is John Rosmer himself, whose own peculiar psychological make-up Freud tends to sideline. Ibsen was gifted in the creation not only of sexually complex and highly charged female character roles, but also in his creation of sexually inhibited men. John Rosmer, like Alfred Allmers in *Little Eyolf*, is sexually repressed, apparently lacking in sexual libido. The cases are not identical. Whilst Allmers is impotent, Rosmer's sexuality is dormant: clearly aroused by Rebecca, he is unwilling to acknowledge it before the play's close. Rosmer's family history is clearly implicated in his sexual reticence. A conservative, patriarchal family, we learn from the housekeeper that in Rosmersholm the children in successive generations have never been known to cry, just as the adults have never been known to laugh. Incapable of proper emotional expression, Rosmer is sexually repressed and it seems likely that the sexual problems encountered in his marriage to Beata may have had their origin in his own lack of libido. Rosmer, like Alfred Allmers, expresses fear of his wife's sexuality:

> ROSMER: . . . Those uncontrollable, sick fits of sensuality – and the way she expected me to reciprocate them. She – frightened me. And then that illogical and remorseless way she reproached herself during those last years.
>
> KROLL: Yes, when she learned she'd never be able to have any children.
>
> ROSMER: Yes, well, I mean – ! To feel such appalling and inescapable anguish about something that was in no way her fault! Is that sanity?
>
> (*R*II, 58–9)

The sexual guilt that leads John Rosmer to commit suicide alongside Rebecca West has two psychological sources. Firstly, as he acknowledges late in the play (it should come as no surprise to the audience), he has sexually desired Rebecca West, and, although he has characteristically suppressed such desire, he realizes that his wife must all along have been conscious of his preference. Secondly, his denial of his wife's probably normal sexual appetite, his possible refusal even to consummate the marriage, could be another source of his feelings of sexual guilt. The childlessness which brought Beata to despair could be understood as an expression of John Rosmer's own sterility; he, not his dead wife, is sexually and psychologically dysfunctional.

Ibsen's dazzling exploration of masculine sexual psychology began in a play written more than twenty years before

Rosmersholm. For, although standard critical accounts regard this play from 1886 as the first in a series of studies in modern psychology, *Rosmersholm* is by no means the first play in which Ibsen experimented with psychological drama. In *Peer Gynt* (1867), that fantastical quest for the 'self', the whole psychological apparatus had already been put in place by Ibsen in a play which quite remarkably anticipates Freud's theory of the unconscious. Ibsen's first major play, *Peer Gynt* predates Freud's early psychological studies by nearly thirty years. Peer Gynt is a young man who is infantilized by his mother and reluctant to leave her apron strings. Clearly terrified – like both John Rosmer and Alfred Allmers – of sexually available young women, the play enacts a series of sexual displacements in which Peer plays out a series of sexual fantasies. These fantasies consist of thoroughly non-realist, dream-like encounters with trolls, sexually voracious mountain girls and seductive desert women. Ibsen's decision, when writing *Peer Gynt*, not to write for the stage – he never really expected it to be performed – meant that he was liberated to explore the boundaries between what we now understand as the conscious and the unconscious.

In the first scene of the play, the young Peer carries his mother across a river on his way to a wedding at which he aims to supplant the groom. He speaks to his mother as a lover, announcing proudly that 'I'm carrying you to my wedding in my arms!' (*PG*I, 38.) Two scenes later, though, he is infantilized when his mother, Aase, threatens to thrash his bottom for misbehaving at the wedding. A partial explanation of the confused, Oedipal relationship between mother and son is provided by Aase's account of her absent husband, a father who:

> had a tongue red for drink.
> An idler he was with his bragging, wasting our wealth,
> Whilst I and my baby sat at home trying to forget.
>
> (*PG*II, 56)

Having been unable to transfer his love from mother to father, Peer remains attached to his mother, and prefers the young virgin, Solveig, with 'psalmbook wrapped in linen/ … cling[ing] to [her] mother's skirt' (*PG*II, 54) to the sexually available Ingrid, whom he has seduced. When Solveig finally leaves her family, ruining her reputation in order to come up to live on the mountainside with Peer Gynt, Peer, although ostensibly welcoming her, is clearly terrified. As soon as Solveig declares herself sexually available in this way, an apparition of an old woman in green rags appears, as if out of Peer's unconscious, and she has with her one whom she claims to be Peer's illegitimate child. She warns Peer that when he kisses Solveig, 'when you'd pet her and play with her,/I'll sit down beside you and demand my share./ She and I will take you by turns' (*PG*III, 82). The old woman's age suggests her as a malevolent mother figure; even though his mother is now dead, it seems Peer is unable to transfer his sexual affections to another woman.

Instead of setting up home with Solveig, Peer Gynt flees. His repressed sexuality is only given expression in the fantastical Troll Scene, in the Hall of the Mountain King (Act II). Peer is invited to be a troll, with all the sexually crude idiosyncrasies that go with troll status – 'Bite him in the bottom!' cry the troll children. The riotous, sexually rampant and vulgar trolls have a lot in common with the Freudian *id*; they are an embodiment of the primitive sexual urges of humans. The trolls represent the *id* untrammelled by the *super-ego* – trolls are men without social and emotional controls.

In his extraordinary anticipation of the Freudian unconscious, and in his invention of the psychological drama, Ibsen's status as one of the great 'modern' playwrights of the late nineteenth century is assured. All of his plays have a powerful psychological dimension. In the very last of these – *When We Dead Awaken* – Ibsen, always keen to innovate and experiment with dramatic form, begins to move beyond realism. It is the move towards new dramatic modes that I will explore in the final chapter.

6

Beyond Realism: *John Gabriel Borkman* and *When We Dead Awaken*

In his dramatic account of John Rosmer's emotional and sexual inhibitions, in *Rosmersholm* (1886), Ibsen revealed himself as brilliant an analyst of masculine as of feminine sexual psychology. His last two plays – *John Gabriel Borkman* (1896) and *When We Dead Awaken* (1899) – greatly extend Ibsen's exploration of the hinterlands of masculine psychology, penetrating its darkest recesses in what must be accounted his gloomiest, most troubling plays. They differ from *Rosmersholm* in important respects, for whereas in the earlier play there remains a socio-political dimension to the drama – the play is partly about the battle between conservative, traditional values and progressive liberalism – in the last two plays Ibsen turns away from the social criticism of his middle period towards a much more intense focus on individual subjectivity. In this respect, and also in terms of the non-realist dramatic modes deployed, both of his last two plays have rather more in common with *Brand* and *Peer Gynt*, plays Ibsen wrote as a young man, than with the dramatic naturalism which brought him both fame and notoriety in the 1870s and 1880s.

Ibsen' s searching analysis of the inner lives of his protagonists in *John Gabriel Borkman* and *When We Dead Awaken*, the emphasis he places on the inner rather than the outer landscapes of human experience, identify him in these final plays with a nascent modernist aesthetic, greatly to be extended in the twentieth century by, amongst others, one of his literary acolytes, James Joyce. The move beyond realism also involves a shift towards symbolic modes of dramatic representation. The shift towards symbolic drama had been clearly announced in *Little Eyolf* (1894), in which the unwelcome rats can be readily identified with Eyolf, the unwanted child, the 'troublesome thing' which the Rat-wife offers to get rid of. The Rat-wife herself is a dream-like figure, a composite character from a fairytale, an emanation of the unconscious, who transforms a dull bourgeois domestic life into a living nightmare. Even before *Little Eyolf*, in *The Lady from the Sea* (1888), the sea symbolically represents freedom and sexual liberty, and Ibsen uses the mermaid myth to structure his account of Ellida's imprisonment in her marriage to Dr Wangel. In *John Gabriel Borkman* and *When We Dead Awaken* the mountains symbolically represent freedom and sexual and emotional fulfilment. At the close of each play the central protagonists make their way up a mountainside to certain death. In climbing the mountain, they leave behind their quotidian lives in a mystical search for the liberty and passionate fulfilment that previously they have sacrificed to their seeking of power and success in other spheres.

Edvard Munch, the Scandinavian artist who produced a lithograph of Ibsen in 1895, described *John Gabriel Borkman* as 'the most powerful winter landscape in Scandinavian art'.[1] It is figuratively, as well as quite literally, a 'winter landscape'. The snowbound mountainside up which Borkman staggers to die, his heart gripped by the icy cold, symbolically corresponds with the freezing over of the tragic hero's heart many years before, when he put worldly success before passionate fulfilment with the woman he loved. *John Gabriel Borkman*, with its dramatic evocation of the darkness, silence and cold of a Norwegian winter, is a sombre survey of a bleakly empty emotional life. It tells the story of a miner's son who becomes a successful financier. Borkman dreams of economic domination of the globe, an idealistic domination in which he would, through his grand enterprises, 'create a sense of fellowship throughout the world' (*B*IV, 198) and 'serve humanity' (*B*II, 154). In order to finance his enterprises, he embezzles money from his bank, intending to pay it back later. The fraud is discovered and he spends eight years in prison. When released, he lives alone in an upstairs room of his house, refusing to see his wife, visited only by an old clerk and his piano-playing daughter, waiting in the conviction – which eventually deserts him – that the 'masses' will demand that he resume his position in the bank in order to 'save' them.

The action of the play begins eight years into Borkman's solitary existence in his single room, alone with his thoughts. We learn during the course of the play that, as a young man, he abandoned Ella Rentheim, the woman he loved, as the price for getting a foot on the professional ladder. Ella, his wife's twin sister, has remained single, fostering Borkman's son during his imprisonment. During the course of the play she comes to upbraid Borkman for his betrayal of her many years before, and begs him to let his son live with her once again, and take her name. Mrs Borkman – who is unforgiving towards her husband, their relationship cold and dead – refuses permission, but Erhart, the son, takes matters into his own hands and seeks out a new life with a woman twice his age. Borkman himself wanders out onto the mountainside, after years of incarceration, and dies.

This is a story of maimed masculinity. John Gabriel Borkman has imagined himself an omnipotent, powerful figure of authority, who would rule the world. Despite his disgrace, he convinces himself that he will be redeemed, so great is the world's need of him:

> BORKMAN: ...The day I am rehabilitated – when they realise they cannot do without me – when they come up to me in this room and get down on their knees and implore me to take over control of the bank again – the new bank they have founded – but cannot run (*stops by the desk as before, and strikes his chest*) I shall stand *here* to receive them. And throughout the land men will ask and learn what conditions John Gabriel Borkman lays down...
>
> ...
>
> BORKMAN: ...Do you know how I sometimes feel?
>
> FOLDAL: How?
>
> BORKMAN: Like a Napoleon maimed in his first battle.
>
> (*BII*, 158–9)

The reference to Napoleon is highly significant, since the French emperor was included in the German philosopher Nietzsche's list of exemplary 'supermen', and this late play by Ibsen would seem to owe not a little to the German philosopher, one of whose main insights into human behaviour was that it is motivated by the will to power. Ibsen was apparently familiar with Nietzsche's work, and contended that he was 'a rare talent who, because of his philosophy, could not be popular in our democratic age'.[2] According to Nietzsche, the masses, whom he termed the herd or mob, conform to tradition, whereas his ideal superman is secure, independent and highly individualistic. The superman is capable of deep feeling, but his passions are rationally controlled. He is a creator of values, a creator of a 'master morality' that reflects the strength and independence of one who is liberated from all values, except those that he deems valid.[3] John Gabriel Borkman is at once the apotheosis of Nietzschean superman and a dramatic representation of the psychologically and emotionally crippling effects of Nietzschean masculinity. Borkman dispenses with conventional values pertaining to fiscal honesty and romantic love. He expresses no remorse for having embezzled money from his bank and for financially ruining hapless small investors such as the loyal Foldal, whom he angrily silences whenever any incidental references to his poverty are made. Such is the heroism and idealism of his grand economic crusade that Borkman feels himself above the morality of the 'masses', not governed by their moral codes, forging his own 'master morality' as part of his grand plan for world domination. Traditional values of romantic love are similarly dispensed with: although Borkman clearly had a passionate regard for Ella Rentheim when he was a young man, he has rationally controlled his feelings for her in pursuit of his ideal of world economic domination. As he explains to his wife, the will to power has been, for him, all-consuming:

> I had the power! And the irresistible calling within me! The buried millions lay there all over the country, deep in the mountains, crying out to me, crying to be released. But no one else hears them. I alone. (*B*III, 178)

Here as elsewhere in the play, the dramatic language has a highly symbolical resonance. For the 'buried millions' that lay 'deep in the mountains' refers, on a literal level, to the iron ore which Borkman wished to mine as part of his global capitalist enterprise. But there is a 'buried' meaning here. The 'millions' that Borkman has left 'buried' symbolically refers to the wealth of human love he has denied in pursuit of power and glory in the masculine sphere. It is this act of denial – the burying of the more 'feminine' part of his psychology – that Ella Rentheim upbraids him with, referring to it as an act of murder:

> ELLA: (*moving closer to him*): You are a murderer! You have committed the mortal sin!
> BORKMAN (*retreats towards the piano*): You are raving, Ella.
> ELLA: You have killed love in me! (*Goes towards him*)...Do you understand what that means?...The sin for which there is no forgiveness is to murder love in a human being.
>
> (*B*II, 169)

In true Nietzschean style, Borkman misogynistically feels he can dispense with women and all that is associated with them: 'Women!' he expostulates to Foldal. 'They corrupt and pervert our lives. They deflect us from our destinies, rob us of our triumphs' (*B*I, 162). And yet it is his denial of the emotional life, a sexually fulfilled life that he could have shared with Ella Rentheim, that maims the very masculinity which Borkman proclaims so ferociously throughout much of the play. For to be a Nietzschean superman is to stand alone, a leader of the masses. In a fleeting moment of optimism, Borkman explains it thus:

> I – I could have created millions! Think of all the mines I could have brought under my control, the shafts I could have sunk. I would have hammered cataracts – hewn quarries. My ships would have covered the world, linking continent to continent. All this I would have created alone. (*B*II, 159)

But, in standing alone, Borkman severs all human connection and the emotional life that goes with it. When Foldal, the failed playwright, reflects of his family that 'None of [them] understand me at all', Borkman's response is that 'That is the curse, the burden we chosen men have to bear. The masses, the mediocre millions – they do not understand us, Vilhelm' (*B*II, 157). Borkman includes one's nearest and dearest in these 'mediocre millions', and, in cutting himself off from the life of the emotions, he has psychologically crippled himself. His is a lonely, isolated masculinity, cut off from the main run of humankind. The desire to 'stand alone'[4] has led to a solipsistic existence, an inability to relate to others which again anticipates the states of consciousness explored by later modernist writers.

Borkman's solipsism is symbolically represented by the room

in which he has voluntarily incarcerated himself, virtually in solitary confinement, for the past eight years. It is only in the walk up to the mountainside with Ella Rentheim, at the close of the play, that Borkman acknowledges the human crime he has committed in renouncing his love for Ella in favour of power and glory in a more masculine sphere. The acknowledgement is all too late though, for, as he himself recognizes, his soul is already dead, murdered at the very moment he deserted Ella Rentheim years before. Ella fears for his health in the cold night air, and he responds that he is already a dead man:

ELLA: It's your health I'm concerned for.
BORKMAN (*laughs*): A dead man's health! You make me laugh.

(*BIV*, 187)

As they stand staring at the mountains together, Borkman comments that his 'treasures' are still buried in the mountains, and he expresses love for them: 'I love you, treasures that crave for life, with your bright retinue of power and glory. I love you, I love you, I love you.' At this point Ella reminds him that he has diverted proper human emotions into the buried earth, emotions that should have been permitted to live above ground:

ELLA: Yes, your love is still buried down there, John. It always has been. But up here, in the daylight, there was a warm, living heart beating for you, and you broke it. Worse, you sold it – for –
BORKMAN (*a cold shiver seems to run through him*): For the Kingdom – and the power – and the glory, you mean? (*BIV*, 199)

It is a 'glory' he never realizes, a glory throttled from its inception by his denial of the more 'feminine' part of his psyche which craves emotional and sexual fulfilment. His death in the icy mountain air is symbolically loaded: 'I think it was the cold that killed him.' Ella reflects, and Mrs Borkman's response is 'The cold? That killed him long ago' (*BIV*, 201).

The central preoccupations of *John Gabriel Borkman* reverberate throughout Ibsen's final play, *When We Dead Awaken*. Arnold Rubek, a world-famous sculptor now on the verge of old age, has, we learn, diverted all the passionate energies of which he is capable into his artistic life, reserving nothing for the flesh-and-blood life of the emotions, denying his own sexuality as well as that of Irene, the woman who was the model for his most famous sculpture, *The Day of Resurrection*. The 'dead' of the play's title are Rubek and Irene, emotionally numbed by the absence of passionate fulfillment in their lives. There is also a sense, though, that Norway itself embodies a living death. The opening dialogue of the play, between Rubek and his wife, the young Maja whom he has tried to use as a substitute for Irene, strongly suggests the death-in-life that is Norway:

> MAJA: Just listen to the silence!
> RUBEK (*smiles indulgently*): Can you hear it?
> MAJA: Hear what?
> RUBEK: The silence.
> MAJA: Certainly I can.
> RUBEK: Perhaps you're right, my dear. One really can hear the silence.
> MAJA: God knows one can. When it's as deafening as it is here –
> RUBEK: Here at the baths, you mean?
> MAJA: Everywhere in Norway. Oh, down in the city it was noisy enough. But even there, I thought that all that noise and bustle had something dead about it.
> RUBEK (*looks hard at her*): Aren't you happy to be home again, Maja?
> MAJA: Are you?
>
> (*WWDAI*, 215–16)

Having spent many years in Germany, it is only on returning to his homeland that Rubek 'awakens' to the fact that he has been living a spiritual and emotional death since Irene left, some years before. Mutually unfulfilled by their marriage, Rubek and Maja confront, in Norway, the emotional wasteland of their lives. But they don't confront it together. Instead, they each meet an alternative partner with whom to share their sense of wasted life. Maja joins up with a mysterious, masterful bear-hunter, whose powerful sexual presence clearly appeals to a young woman who, it is clear, is far from sexually satisfied with her husband. Rubek himself is astonished to be confronted, at the spa hotel in which they are staying, by Irene herself. Irene, it transpires, went mad when she left him, and it quickly becomes clear that the emotional intimacy she enjoyed with Rubek has been destroyed for ever by the mental instability she now endures. She is tended by a nun who never lets her out of her sight, and her disordered thoughts and the obvious desire she has to kill Rubek – she frequently pulls a knife on him when he is not looking, which greatly adds to the dramatic tension of the play – mean that the youthful bond she had with the sculptor can never be properly recovered.

That Rubek is to blame for Irene's broken mind becomes evident in the earliest of their exchanges. Utterly inspired by Irene as his model, he deliberately severed himself from her as a living, breathing and sexual being:

IRENE: . . . You wronged my inmost being.

RUBEK: I?

IRENE: Yes, you. I stripped myself naked for you to gaze at me. (*More quietly.*) And you never once touched me. . . .

RUBEK: Before all else I was an artist. And I was sick – sick with a longing to create the one great work of my life. It was to be called: 'The Day of Resurrection'.

(*WWDAI*, 232)

There is a clear parallel between Irene's situation, here, and that of Ella Rentheim, in *John Gabriel Borkman*. In each play, the leading male protagonist has diverted all available emotional energy into ideal, abstract projects, denying the flesh-and-blood relationships available to him. Such denial, in *When We Dead Awaken* as in *John Gabriel Borkman*, leads to sexual and emotional paralysis and spiritual death. Rubek used life – his and Irene's emotional life – as material for his art. He poured his and Irene's soul into his art when he should, he acknowledges late in his life, have focused instead on *living*, on life itself. His sacrifice of his and Irene's emotional and sexual life to his sculpture eventually kills both of them. But their bodily death is registered in the play as a mere epilogue to the spiritual and emotional death which took place years before. Only when they are on the top of the mountain which they climb together can they temporarily transcend the living death of Norway, the living death of the lives to which they had been subjected through Rubek's commitment to his art.

Irene has been imprisoned in a lunatic asylum, which becomes in the play a symbol for a more general sense of spiritual, mental and emotional confinement. Rubek's 'prison' is self-imposed, the jailhouse of artistic endeavour. Rubek's most famous sculpture – *The Day of Resurrection* – symbolically expresses his emotional apprehension of his wasted life. An awakened young woman occupies the middle ground of the sculpture, whilst 'In the foreground, beside a spring, as it might be here, there sits a man weighed down by guilt; he cannot free himself from the earth's crust. I call him remorse – remorse for a forfeited life', (*WWDA*II, 251). This play, like *John Gabriel Borkman* before it, explores a maimed masculine subjectivity, its self-inflicted wounds destroying also the women with whom it has made contact.

In the play's extraordinarily brief final act, Rubek and Irene walk to the top of the mountain together in search of the 'glory of the world...from the top of a mountain' he had once promised her (*WWDA*II, 254). Irene confesses to Rubek that she has contemplated killing him earlier that day:

> RUBEK: Why didn't you?
> IRENE: I suddenly realised that you were already dead. You'd been dead for years.
> RUBEK: Dead?
> IRENE: Dead. Like me...
> RUBEK: I don't call that death....
> IRENE: Then where is the burning passion you fought against when I stood naked before you as the woman rising from the dead?...Too late. Too late....The desire to live died in me, Arnold.
>
> (*WWDA*III, 265)

Irene and Rubek decide to spend one hour of 'life' on the mountain top before perishing in the storm. On their way to the summit, they are engulfed by an avalanche. The avalanche in the third and final act of *When We Dead Awaken* is not readily stageable, and is certainly far removed from the domestic realism of Ibsen's middle-period dramas. The third act is dramatized altogether outside of domestic spaces, up on the top of a cold mountain. This is entirely appropriate. Rubek and his wife, Maja, have fled from their luxurious villa in Germany, where they felt themselves to be withering away on the vine of an unfulfilled bourgeois domestic existence. None the less, neither this play nor *John Gabriel Borkman* before it has entirely eschewed the dramatic realism for which Ibsen is best known and for which he was fêted during his lifetime. Rubek's and Maja's dissection of their marriage relation, and his and Irene's remorseful and mournful contemplation of the passionate sexual fulfilment they never enjoyed together, would have been immediately recognized and appreciated by those theatre audiences who watched *A Doll's House* and *Little Eyolf*. It is Ibsen's relentless scrutiny of individual subjectivities in these late plays, and his increasing deployment of symbolic modes of representation with an attendant heightened poetic language which differentiates them from the dramatic output of his middle period.

It is difficult not to infer an autobiographical context for both of these plays. Ibsen, once so obscure, was much fêted when he returned to Norway after his long, self-imposed exile in Germany and Italy. But his joy at the homage that was paid was tempered by a feeling that his emotional life was not all that it might have been. He and his wife Suzannah spent longer periods apart than they had ever done before their return to their homeland, and Ibsen embroiled himself in hopeless, doomed (and almost certainly sexless) relationships with young women who would not have given him a second glance had he not been Ibsen the playwright. Ibsen, like Arnold Rubek, felt he had poured the best part of his life into his art. From the vantage point of the late twentieth century, the immensity of the body of work he produced, and the profound influence he exerted on late-Victorian and early modernist culture, more than compensate for any losses in his emotional life. But it is, possibly, those very losses which inform the bleakly powerful emotional landscapes of his last two plays.

7

Afterword: Ibsen Now

One hundred years after Ibsen's death, his plays remain as popular in Britain as when they first arrived on the London stage in 1889. He is, too, the most frequently televised dramatist after Shakespeare. Both the realism of Ibsen's middle drama – the stifling drawing-room settings of *A Doll's House*, *Ghosts* and *Hedda Gabler* – and the more existential modernity of the late plays such as *John Gabriel Borkman* and *When We Dead Awaken*, continue to appeal to twenty-first century theatre audiences accustomed equally to theatrical naturalism and to modernist experimentation. That Ibsen's dramatic realism retained its power at the end of the 1990s was amply demonstrated by London's Playhouse 1997 production of *A Doll's House*, starring Janet McTeer. The 'prop-rich' conventions of the nineteenth-century stage, along with Ibsen's detailed and painstaking *mise en scène*, were faithfully reproduced – there was nothing remotely avant-gardist about the production. And yet the tension in the theatre was palpable, with a significant proportion of the audience visibly moved by the final dialogue between Nora and Torvald Helmer in which the wreckage of their marriage is surveyed with a quiet agony. Into the twenty-first century the Greenwich Playhouse's production of *A Doll's House* (December 2004–January 2005) was equally faithful in its naturalistic recreation of the late-nineteenth century bourgeois household, with its delicately decorated Christmas tree and close attention to costume detail. Alice Grace's stunning performance as a beautifully complex Nora, whose fragility and seeming subservience only thinly veil her exceptional strength and moral fibre, was complemented by Martin Beere's moving rendition of Dr Rank's hopeless love for the unhappy young wife.

The intense theatricality inherent in Ibsen's plays is the source of their continued vigour and variety in production. The ascendancy of the modernist aesthetic in the early-twentieth century, which continued to influence late-twentieth century theatre, has meant that avant-gardist directors have sometimes tried to re-invent Ibsen's realism along modernist lines, emphasizing the psychological and existential dimensions of his work rather than the social and material relationships through which wider human issues are explored in the plays. One example of a number of such productions was Ingmar Bergman's 1964 production of *Hedda Gabler* in the Royal Dramatic Theatre in Stockholm. Ignoring Ibsen's detailed staging instructions, Bergman freed the play of its naturalistic, material details – the carpets, the bric-à-brac, the piano, and other domestic paraphernalia – and presented the audience instead with a fully enclosed, dark red space on the stage, thereby invoking the mood of suffocation and leaden emptiness which dominates the play.[1] Not all critics have welcomed such departures from Ibsen's thoroughly material and particularized brand of realism. Charles Marowitz, for example, denounced Bergman's approach, arguing that the only proper style of production suited to Ibsen's plays is 'the most diligent application of Stanislavsky-based realism',[2] and this has, in fact, remained the approach favoured by most directors.

Ibsen's concern with the position of women in society, and with the tensions and stresses within middle-class marriage, has guaranteed his continued popularity in Western Europe and the USA into the late-twentieth and twenty-first centuries when women's issues have frequently taken centre stage in the political and cultural arena. Memorable performances of his women's roles by well-known actresses such as Juliet Stevenson, Diana Rigg and Glenda Jackson in the second half of the twentieth century consolidated Ibsen's popularity, and his plays continue to create outstanding opportunities for women in London's theatres. The number of feminist literary-critical responses to his work has continued to grow, and has ensured that his 'blue-stocking' reputation has persisted.[3] London's Comedy Theatre production of *Ghosts* in April–June 2001 presented in Mrs Alving – who is more usually performed as an embittered widow and controlling mother – a vulnerable, introspective lead female role. Richard Eyre's dazzling production of *Hedda Gabler* at the Almeida (spring 2005) created in Eve Best's account of the female lead a darkly ironic role. Aware of life's absurdity and viewing it with an admixture of gloomy humour and angry exasperation, Best's sharp-featured Hedda rivalled all earlier performances.

The more recent late-twentieth and twenty-first century concern with the faultlines, stresses and strains within traditional concepts of masculinity will, I believe, further sustain the cultural power of Ibsen's plays, in which masculine heroes are few, and sympathetic male characters are tentative and uncertain of themselves, challenging those dominant nineteenth-century discourses on masculinity which constructed the active, rational and commanding male as the ideal archetype.

The rise of 'Green' politics in the late-twentieth century has also given a new lease of life to *An Enemy of the People*, in which Dr Stockmann can readily be appropriated as a proto-environmentalist. Until recently the sheer number of bit part players required for the crowd scenes in this play has meant that it has been relatively rarely performed. The hugely successful 1998 production of the play in London's National Theatre, starring Ian McKellan, indicated the topicality of this play's themes at the turn of the twenty-first century.

That Ibsen – who, as I have already remarked, never set foot on British soil – has been thoroughly assimilated into British cultural life, is confirmed by the appearance of *A Doll's House* as a 'set text' on Advanced Level English Literature syllabuses. The Norwegian temper and ambience of his plays, which should never be overlooked, did not prevent his late-Victorian aficionados – Bernard Shaw, Edmund Gosse and Eleanor Marx – from claiming him as their own. Over a hundred years later the same can be said for his enormous readership and theatrical following in twenty-first-century Britain.

Notes

CHAPTER 1. IBSENISM AND *A DOLL'S HOUSE*

1 George Bernard Shaw, 'Fragments of a Fabian Lecture, 1890', British Library Add. MS 50661, quoted in J. L. Wiesenthal, *Shaw and Ibsen* (Toronto, Buffalo and London, 1979), 81.
2 Edith Lees Ellis, *Stories and Essays* (1914), 128.
3 Norman and Jean MacKenzie, *The First Fabians* (London, 1979), 167.
4 Yvonne Kapp, *Eleanor Marx*, vol. 2 (London, 1976), 103.
5 David Rubinstein, *Before the Suffragettes* (Brighton, 1986), 24.
6 Clement Scott, unsigned notice of *A Doll's House* in the *Daily Telegraph*, 8 June 1889, 3.
7 Clement Scott, 'A Doll's House', *Theatre*, 14 (July 1889), 19–22.
8 William Archer, *Theatre*, 3 (April 1884), 209–14.
9 See Michael Meyer, *Henrik Ibsen: The Farewell to Poetry, 1864–1882* (London, 1971), 250–52.
10 Meyer, *Farewell to Poetry*, 266.
11 Meyer, *Farewell to Poetry*, 254.
12 Meyer, *Farewell to Poetry*, 261.
13 Walter Besant, 'The Doll's House – and After', *English Illustrated Magazine* (January 1890), 315–25, quote from p. 320.
14 Besant, 'The Doll's House – and After', 325.
15 George Bernard Shaw, 'Still After the Doll's House: A Sequel to Mr. Besant's Sequel to Henrik Ibsen's Play', *Time* (February 1890), 197–207.

CHAPTER 2. IBSEN, REALISM AND 'MODERN' DRAMA: FROM NORWEGIAN NATIONALISM TO *GHOSTS*

1 Björnstjerne Björnson (1832–1910) was very influential in the establishment of an indigenous Norwegian literature: his 1857 novel, *Sunny Hill*, was a realistic treatment of peasant life. He was also a powerful leader in the political struggle that led to the

establishment of Norway as an independent country in 1905. His success as a writer was more immediate than Ibsen's, and although Björnson quite often gave Ibsen financial help, and they admired each other's work, Ibsen's increasing scepticism towards Norwegian nationalism as he grew older meant that their friendship was not always easy. It did, though, endure.

2 *The Feast at Solhaug* (1855) was full of echoes of M. B. Landstal's recently collected Norwegian folk ballads (1853). See Michael Meyer, *Henrik Ibsen: The Making of a Dramatist 1828–1864* (London, 1967), 142–3.

3 Meyer, *Making of a Dramatist*, 175.

4 Meyer, *Making of a Dramatist*, 182.

5 Camilla Collett, *The Judge's Daughters* (1854–5), quoted in Meyer, *Making of a Dramatist*, 217.

6 Henrik Ibsen, speech in Copenhagen, 1 April 1898, quoted in Meyer, *Making of a Dramatist*, 238.

7 Ibsen, letter to Hegel, 31 October 1868. Quoted in Michael Meyer, *Henrik Ibsen: The Farewell to Poetry*, 1864–1882, (London, 1971), 85.

8 Ibsen, letter to Hegel, 85.

9 Ibsen, letter to Hegel, 101.

10 Henry James, 'On the Occasion of *Hedda Gabler*', *New Review*, (4 June 1891), 519–30. Quoted extracts are from a reprint of the essay in Michael Egan (ed.), *Ibsen: The Critical Heritage* (London, 1972), 237 and 239.

11 Meyer, *Farewell to Poetry*, 261.

12 Meyer, *Farewell to Poetry*, 191.

13 *Ibsen, Letters and Speeches*, ed. and trans. Evert Sprinchorn (New York, 1964), 222.

14 *Ibsen, Letters and Speeches*, 300.

15 George Bernard Shaw, 'The Quintessence of Ibsenism', in J. L. Wiesenthal (ed.), *Shaw and Ibsen* (Toronto, Buffalo and London, 1979), 140.

16 Max Nordau, *Degeneration* (1892; Lincoln and London, 1993), 350.

17 Nordau, *Degeneration*, 352.

18 Meyer, *Farewell to Poetry*, 299.

19 *Daily Telegraph*, 14 March 1891.

20 Meyer, *Farewell to Poetry*, 296–7.

CHAPTER 3. LIBERALISM AND ITS DISCONTENTS: IBSEN'S POLITICS IN *AN ENEMY OF THE PEOPLE*

1 Michael Meyer, *Henrik Ibsen: The Farewell to Poetry, 1864–1882* (London, 1971), 68.

2 Meyer, *Farewell to Poetry*, 309.
3 Letter to Hegel, 9 September 1882, quoted in Meyer, *Farewell to Poetry*, 308.
4 Raymond Williams, *Modern Tragedy* (2nd ed., London, 1979), 101.
5 I owe this insight to Helge Ronning's 'Individualism and the Liberal Dilemma: Notes towards a Sociological Interpretation of *An Enemy of the People*', in Harald Noreng *et al.* (eds.), *Contemporary Approaches to Ibsen* (Oslo, Bergen and Tromso, 1977).
6 Quoted in Michael Meyer's Introduction to *An Enemy of the People* in *Ibsen, Plays Two* (London, 1992), 112.
7 Max Nordau, *Degeneration* (1895: Lincoln and London, 1993), 357.

CHAPTER 4. IBSEN'S WOMEN: *THE LADY FROM THE SEA, HEDDA GABLER* AND *LITTLE EYOLF*

1 James Joyce, 'Ibsen's New Drama', *Fortnightly Review*, new series 67 (1 April 1990), 575–90. Quoted in Michael Egan, *Ibsen: The Critical Heritage* (London, 1972), 388.
2 Louie Bennett, 'Ibsen as a Pioneer of the Woman Movement', *Westminster Review*, 173 (1910), 278–85, quote from p. 278.
3 Quoted in Gail Finney, 'Ibsen and Feminism', in James McFarlane (ed.), *Cambridge Companion to Ibsen* (Cambridge, 1994), 89–105, p. 90. I am indebted to Finney's essay for this and some of the other source material in this chapter.
4 See Mary Morison, *The Correspondence of Henrik Ibsen* (New York, 1970), 365, 423–4.
5 Michael Meyer, *Henrik Ibsen: The Making of a Dramatist, 1828–1864* (London, 1967), 146.
6 Elizabeth Robins, *Ibsen and the Actress* (1928; New York, 1973).
7 Of the so-called English-language 'New Woman' writers of the period, only George Egerton, in her *Keynotes* and *Discords* (1893 and 1894) matches Ibsen's sympathetic treatment of female sexuality.
8 Unsigned Notice of *The Lady from the Sea*, *Referee* (17 May 1891), 2. Quoted in Michael Egan, *Ibsen: The Critical Heritage* (London, 1972), 250.
9 Quoted in Michael Meyer, Introduction to *Hedda Gabler*, in *Ibsen, Plays Two* (London, 1992), 233.
10 Michael Billington, *Guardian*, 5 September 1991, reviewing a 1991 Dublin production of *Hedda Gabler*.

CHAPTER 5. IBSEN, FREUD AND PSYCHOLOGICAL DRAMA: *ROSMERSHOLM* AND *PEER GYNT*

1 'Notes Upon a Case of Obsessional Neurosis' (1909), *The Standard Edition of the Complete Psychological Works of Sigmund Freud*, trans. and ed. James Strachey, vol. 10 (London 1964), 215.
2 By 'realist' character I refer to a method of characterization, common in both the nineteenth-century novel and in Ibsen's middle plays, which focuses on readily recognizable, socially representative 'types'. Realist characters can be fully explained by authors and rationally apprehended by readers.
3 Quoted in Michael Meyer, Introduction to *Rosmersholm*, in *Ibsen, Plays Three* (London, 1995), 22.
4 Unsigned notice in *The Times*, 24 February 1891, 10. Quoted in Michael Egan, *Ibsen: The Critical Heritage* (London, 1972), 163.
5 Unsigned notice by Clement Scott in the *Daily Telegraph*, 24 February 1891, 3. Quoted in Egan, *The Critical Heritage*, 167–8.
6 Sigmund Freud, 'Some Character Types Met with in Psycho-Analytic Work' (1916), repr. in James McFarlane (ed.), *Henrik Ibsen*, Penguin Critical Anthologies (Harmondsworth, 1970), 392–9.
7 Freud, 'Some Character Types', 395.
8 Freud, 'Some Character Types', 396.

CHAPTER 6. BEYOND REALISM: *JOHN GABRIEL BORKMAN* AND *WHEN WE DEAD AWAKEN*

1 Quoted in Michael Meyer, *Henrik Ibsen, The Top of a Cold Mountain, 1883–1906* (London, 1971), 268.
2 Quoted in Meyer, *Top of a Cold Mountain*, 319.
3 See especially Friedrich Nietzsche, *Beyond Good and Evil* (1886), *Ecce Homo* (1886) and *The Will to Power* (1901).
4 The final words of Dr Stockman ('The strongest man is he who stands alone'), in *An Enemy of the People*, are appropriate here, as Ibsen's earlier protagonist is a more genial forerunner of the sombre Borkman.

CHAPTER 7. AFTERWORD: IBSEN NOW

1 For a description of this and many other productions of Ibsen's plays in the twentieth century, see Frederick K. Marker and Lise-Lone

Marker, 'Ibsen and the Twentieth-Century Stage', in James McFarlane (ed.), *Cambridge Companion to Ibsen* (Cambridge, 1994), 183–204.

2 Charles Marowitz, *Confessions of a Counterfeit Critic* (London, 1973), 170.

3 See bibliography for a number of feminist readings of Ibsen's plays.

Select Bibliography

PLAYS BY HENRIK IBSEN (IN CHRONOLOGICAL ORDER)

Catiline (1850)
The Burial Mound (1850)
St John's Night (1853)
Lady Inger of Ostraat (1855)
The Feast of Solhaug (1856)
Olaf Liljekrans (1857)
The Vikings at Helgeland (1858)
Love's Comedy (1862)
The Pretenders (1863)
Brand (1866)
Peer Gynt (1867)
The League of Youth (1869)
Emperor and Galilean (1873)
The Pillars of Society (1877)
A Doll's House (1879)
Ghosts (1881)
An Enemy of the People (1882)
The Wild Duck (1884)
Rosmersholm (1886)
The Lady From the Sea (1888)
Hedda Gabler (1890)
The Master Builder (1892)
Little Eyolf (1894)
John Gabriel Borkman (1896)
When We Dead Awaken (1899)

OTHER TEXTS BY IBSEN

Poems (1871)

Ibsen's Letters and Speeches, edited by Evert Sprinchorn (London, 1965). A wonderful book of source material, much of it eminently quotable. Includes Ibsen's pronouncements on the Women's Movement and Socialism.

TRANSLATIONS

McFarlane, James, *The Oxford Ibsen*, 8 vols. (Oxford, 1960–77). This is the single most comprehensive reference work for the English-speaking student of Ibsen's plays. Includes translations of all Ibsen's plays by McFarlane and others.

Meyer, Michael, *Ibsen: Plays*, 6 vols. Methuen Drama (London, 1980–87). Reliable and accessible translations of Ibsen's sixteen best-known plays, with informative critical introductions.

BIBLIOGRAPHIES AND WORKS OF REFERENCE

Bryan, George B., *An Ibsen Companion: A Dictionary Guide to the Life, Works and Critical Reception of Henrik Ibsen* (Westport, Conn., 1984). A useful quick-reference guide.

McFarlane, James, *The Oxford Ibsen*, 8 vols. (Oxford, 1960–77). This provides extensive bibliographical information up to 1977. Essential reading.

Meyer, Michael, *Ibsen: A Bibliography* (Harmondsworth, 1985). Essential for any research student.

Meyer, Michael, *Ibsen on File* (London, 1985). Useful quick-reference guide.

BIOGRAPHICAL/CONTEXTUAL STUDIES

Ferguson, Robert, *Henrik Ibsen: A New Biography* (London, 1996). Adds very little to Meyer's vivid three-volume account of Ibsen's life and work, which I prefer.

McFarlane, James, *Ibsen and the Temper of Norwegian Literature* (London, 1960). Conveys a strong sense of the intellectual and cultural context of Ibsen's dramatic output.

Meyer, Michael, *Ibsen: A Biography*, 3 vols. (London, 1967–70; published in a single volume, London 1971). Provides a very strong sense of the texture of Ibsen's lived experience as a man and as a dramatist. Not speculative, but very sound, full and reliable.

IBSEN'S CRITICAL RECEPTION IN BRITAIN

Ibsen's plays made such a great impact on late-Victorian British culture and intellectual life that a whole sub-area of study has grown up around it.

Egan, Michael, *Ibsen: The Critical Heritage* (London, 1972). This is an invaluable source for most of the contemporary responses to Ibsen in the late nineteenth and early twentieth centuries, and includes some of the items listed immediately below.

Aveling, Edward, '"Nora" and "Breaking a Butterfly"', *Today*, 1 (1884), 473–80.

Baylen, Joseph O., 'Edmund Gosse, William Archer, and Ibsen in Late Victorian Britain', *Tennessee Studies in Literature*, 20 (1975), 124ff.

Bennett, Louie, 'Ibsen as a Pioneer of the Woman Movement' *Westminster Review*, 173 (1910), 278–85.

Britain, Ian, 'Bernard Shaw, Ibsen, and the Ethics of English Socialism' *Victorian Studies*, 21:3 (1978) 381–401.

Britain, Ian, 'A Transplanted Doll's House: Ibsenism, Feminism and Socialism in Late-Victorian and Edwardian England', in Ian Donaldson (ed.), *Transformations in Modern European Drama* (London and Basingstoke, 1983).

Bulan, Swanhilde, 'A Doll's House Revisited', *Votes for Women* (17 February 1911), 8.

Dukore, Bernard E., 'Karl Marx's Youngest Daughter and *A Doll's House*', *Theatre Journal*, 42: 3 (October 1990), 308–21.

Ellis, Havelock, 'Women and Socialism', *Today*, I (1884), 362–3. Interesting discussion of *A Doll's House*.

Gilliland, Mary S., 'Ibsen's Women, a Lecture' (London, 1894).

Gosse, Edmund, *Ibsen* (London, 1907).

James, Henry, 'On the Occasion of *Hedda Gabler*', *New Review* (1891). Repr. in James McFarlane (ed.), *Henrik Ibsen: A Critical Anthology*, Penguin Critical Anthologies (Harmondsworth, 1970).

Joyce, James, 'When We Dead Awaken', *Fortnightly Review*, 73 (1900), 575–90. Joyce was one of the few contemporary critics (others included Shaw) to perceive the innovative qualities of Ibsen's final play.

May, Keith M., *Ibsen and Shaw* (New York, 1985).

Nordau, Max, 'Ibsen', in *Degeneration* (New York, 1895). One of Ibsen's bitterest enemies, this is a vituperative but interesting attack on Ibsen's 'degenerative' plays.

Postlewait, Thomas, *Prophet of the New Drama: William Archer and the Ibsen Campaign* (Westport, Conn., 1985).

Postlewait, Thomas, (ed.), *William Archer on Ibsen: The Major Essays, 1889–1919* (Westport, Conn. and London, 1984).

Robins, Elizabeth, *Ibsen and the Actress* (London, 1928). This was given as a lecture before the Royal Society of Arts, under the auspices of the British Drama League, March 12 1928. Robins was a notable performer of Ibsen's female roles in London in the 1890s and beyond. One gets a very powerful sense here of the extent to which Ibsen's plays opened up a whole new theatrical world for female actresses as well as audiences.

Shaw, George Bernard, *The Quintessence of Ibsenism* (London, 1891).

Shaw, George Bernard, *The Quintessence of Ibsenism, Now Completed to the Death of Ibsen* (London, 1913).

Wiesenthal, J.L. (ed. and intro.) *Shaw and Ibsen: Bernard Shaw's The Quintessence of Ibsenism and Related Writings* (Toronto, Buffalo and London, 1979). Contains original material which is otherwise difficult to access, including a fragment from Shaw's Fabian Lecture on Ibsen.

CRITICAL READINGS

Ackley, Katherine Anne, 'A Rage to Live: The Violent Life and Death of Hedda Gabler', in Katherine Anne Ackley (ed.), *Women and Violence in Literature: An Essay Collection* (New York, 1990).

Behrendt, Patricia Flanagan, 'The Narcissus Paradigm in Hedda Gabler', *The Journal of Evolutionary Psychology*, 6 (1985), 202–10.

Bjorby, Pal, Dvergsdal, Alvhild, and Stegane, Idar (eds), *Ibsen on the Cusp of the 21st Century: Critical Perspectives* (Laksevag, Norway, 2005). A substantial and important recent collection of critical essays covering the full range of Ibsen's *œuvre*.

Cameron, Deborah, 'Ibsen and British Women's Drama', *Ibsen Studies*, 4:1 (2004), 92–102.

D'Heurle, A. and Feimer, J. N. 'Lost Children: the Role of the Child in the Psychological Plays of Henrik Ibsen', *Psychoanalysis Review*, 63 (1976), 27–47.

Ewbank, Inga-Stina, 'Ibsen and the Language of Women', in Mary Jacobus (ed.), *Women Writing and Writing About Women* (London, 1979), 114–32. This is an important contribution to the growing body of critical literature on Ibsen and women.

Farfan, Penny, *Women, Modernism and Performance* (Cambridge and New York, 2004). Identifies Ibsen as a central figure in the development of feminist modernism.

Freud, Sigmund, 'Notes Upon a case of Obsessional Neurosis' (1909), in James Strachey (trans. and ed.), *Standard Edition of the Complete Works of Sigmund Freud*, vol. 10 (London, 1964).

Freud, Sigmund, 'Some Character Types Met With in Psycho-Analytic Work' (1916), in James Strachey (trans. and ed.), *Standard Edition of the Complete Works of Sigmund Freud*, vol. 14. More readily available in James McFarlane, *Henrik Ibsen, A Critical Anthology* (Harmondsworth, 1970). Freud's essay includes the first full-length psychoanalytical reading of a play by Ibsen (he interrogates Rebecca West's inexplicable rejection of John Rosmer in *Rosmersholm*). It remains convincing today.

Hartman, Ellen, 'Ibsen's Motherless Women', *Ibsen Studies*, 4:1 (2004), 80–91.

Helland, Frode, 'Petrified Time: Ibsen's Response to Modernity With Special Emphasis on *Little Eyolf*', *Ibsen Studies*, 3:2 (2003), 135–44.

Johnsen, William A., *Violence and Modernism: Ibsen, Joyce and Woolf* (Gainesville, Florida, 2003). Situates Ibsen's drama in the modernist canon.

Konrad, Linn B., 'Father's Sins and Mother's Guilt: Dramatic Responses to Darwin', in James Redmond (ed.), *Drama, Sex and Politics* (Cambridge, 1985).

Lanlan, Xie, 'Peer Gynt's Female World', *Ibsen Studies*, 5:2 (2005), 172–79.

McFarlane, James, *Cambridge Companion to Ibsen* (Cambridge, 1994). This is easily the best late-twentieth century English-language account of Ibsen's work. It includes essays on the full range of his dramatic output – early historical dramas, his works of social realism, his relation to feminism, his middle and late plays – as well as accounts of his poetry and his relationship to the development of modern European theatre. There are also essays on Ibsen on the twentieth-century stage and on Ibsen, film and television, as well as two useful bibliographical chapters.

McFarlane, James, *Ibsen and Meaning: Studies, Essays & Prefaces, 1953–87* (Norwich, 1989). Along with Michael Meyer, McFarlane is the most comprehensive and knowledgeable of Ibsen's critics in England in the second half of the twentieth century. This collection of McFarlane's critical writings on the Norwegian playwright is wide-ranging and acute.

McFarlane, James, *Henrik Ibsen, A Critical Anthology* (Harmondsworth, 1970). A wonderful anthology, ranging from contemporary reviews to more recent critical accounts. Includes Freud's psychoanalytic reading of *Rosmersholm* as well as Henry James's enthusiastic response to *Hedda Gabler*.

Orjasaeter, Kristin, 'Mother, Wife and Role Model: A Contextual Perspective on Feminism in *A Doll's House*', *Ibsen Studies*, 5:1 (2005), 19-47.

Schanke, Robert A., *Ibsen in America: A Century of Change* (London, 1988). Includes a quite interesting discussion of Ibsen's meaning for women and feminism.

Sprinchorn, Evert, 'Syphilis in Ibsen's Ghosts', *Ibsen Studies*, 4:2 (2004), 191-204.

Templeton, Joan, 'The Doll's House Backlash: Criticism, Feminism, and Ibsen', *PMLA (Publications of the Modern Language Association of America)*, 104, 1 (1989), 28–40.

Velissarious, A. 'Mental Illness and the Problem of Female Identity in Ibsen', in James Redmond (ed.), *Madness in Drama* (Cambridge 1993).

Index